CALIFORNIA TENANTS' HANDBOOK

by California attorneys

Myron Moskovitz
Ralph Warner
Charles E. Sherman

Edited by Toni Lynne Ihara
Illustrations by Linda Allison
Design and typography by
Nancy Kleban and Michael Meyer

NOLO PRESS
Courtyard Books
Berkeley • Occidental
P.O. Box 544, Occidental, Ca. 95465

PRINTING HISTORY

First Edition	
First printing	August 1972
Second printing	January 1973
Second Edition	
First printing	May 1974
Second printing (revised)	February 1975.
Third Edition	
First Printing	November 1975
Second Printing	April 1976
Fourth Edition	
First Printing	January 1977
Second Printing (revised)	December 1977

THE TREASURE CHAMBER

We wish to thank the following people associated with the first Moskovitz manuscript: Pedro Echeverria and Ronald Vera for their research assistance, Mary Durant and Madeline Finlay for their secretarial assistance, Allan David Heskin for his editorial assistance and Ann Curtis for her artwork.

We also wish to express our gratitude to some friends who helped to make this a better book. Thanks to Lucretia Edwards, Jeffrey Carter, Alan Verson, Paul Rosenthal, Carmen Massey and especially to Geri Brown, who did the index.

ISBN 0-917316-11-8

TABLE OF CONTENTS

INTRODUCTION

The purpose of this handbook is to inform you, the California tenant, of your legal and practical rights. We aim here to simplify, to speak plainly to those who do not have legal training. As an informed tenant you can do a great deal to avoid problems with your landlord. As an informed tenant, there is much you can do to intelligently handle those problems that can't be avoided.

This book is not meant to completely replace lawyers. There are times when it would be wise to consult a lawyer expert in the area of landlord-tenant law. These occasions will be indicated throughout this handbook. We believe, however, that after reading this book you will be better able to protect yourself when dealing with your landlord, and able to avoid many problems before they happen.

It is important to understand at the outset that California law is favorable to landlords. The deck is stacked against the tenant. In most situations you will find that the legislature has given your landlord a lot of protection while giving you very little. We can't magically re-stack the deck in this small book. We can, and do, give you a lot of information that will even the odds a little.

There are some who will feel that this book is overly biased in favor of tenants and that the existence of bad tenants and good landlords is overlooked. To this charge we plead guilty. In these pages the landlord tends rather regularly to seem like an ogre. This does not mean that we preach that "badness" is necessarily in the nature of landlords, but, since this book is about problems seen from the tenant's point of view, we do focus upon all the foul deeds that landlords have been known to do. Yes, this book is purposely oriented around tenant's problems. Landlords have associations, lobbyists, lawyers and legislators to protect their interests, while tenants have almost no resources.* This book is designed to change this imbalance. In short—this is a battle book.

It has to be said somewhere where it will stand out, so why not here: The heart of the tenant's problem is not the laws and regulations (imperfect though they may be), nor the goodness or badness of landlords (for they, like you, are but human)—no, the heart of the problem is with the supply of housing. It is drastically short. No matter how well you represent yourself, no matter how much the rules become improved, no matter how together tenants become, the basic rules of supply and demand will still allow landlords to rule the roost. Huge sums of public money are being spent daily, hourly, to feed the big machines that suck us all dry; but very little of that money ever sees its way into the life of the average person, and we fall pathetically short of all of our potentials for domestic harmony. If there were enough good places to go around, then many of the problems that this book is about would disappear as if by magic. That being said, we must move on, for nothing we can say here will immediately increase the housing supply, and there are some immediate tasks to be accomplished in the rest of these pages.

---

*There is some hope that this imbalance will change. In 1977 a new statewide group was formed to represent and stand up for tenants. It's called the California Housing Action and Information Network (CHAIN). For more information, and to get a copy of the CHAIN newletter, write P. O. Box 2103, Sacramento, CA. 94810. If you can afford a small donation, send it along.

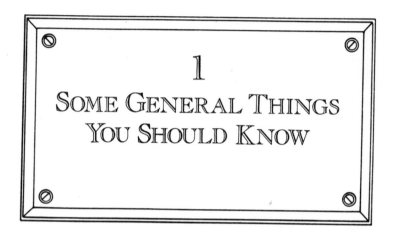

1

SOME GENERAL THINGS
YOU SHOULD KNOW

A. WHO IS YOUR LANDLORD?

Know Your Landlord.[*] Your landlord may be a little old man with a Siamese cat and a bad head for arithmetic or you may rent from a large corporation. There is no typical landlord. In this book we give you a lot of information about your legal rights, but we can't tell you what kind of a landlord you have. It is extremely important that you find out what kind of person your landlord is, because having complete knowledge of your legal rights will help you very little if you lack a good human understanding of the person with whom you are dealing. Coupled with such an understanding this book can be of great value.

Along with understanding the personality of your landlord, it is important to know his problems, his circumstances and his style of operating. Dealing with a retired lady managing her late uncle's duplex will obviously be a lot different from dealing with an institution with 500 units, managers, rules and red tape.

---

[*]Of course, it is equally fair to say to a landlord "know your tenant and your legal rights". There is an excellent book available for landlords entitled *Landlording*. See the back of this book for a description.

Know Your Manager. Many medium to large apartment complexes have managers. The landlord wants to make money, but he wants somebody else to do the dirty work of actually managing the rental property. More and more landlords are hiring management corporations who specialize in managing lots of rental units and who get paid a percentage (about 10%) of the rental income. Such companies tend to be sticklers for rules and procedures, but are usually less emotionally involved than landlords, and are often more rational at arriving at business-like compromises.* Often, however, the landlord will simply give a student or older person free or reduced rent to look after his property on a part time basis. Just as there are all sorts of landlords there is an equal variety of managers.

In dealing with your manager on a day to day basis, it is important not only to notice who he is and how best to deal with him; it is also important to notice his relationship to the landlord. Remember, the landlord and the manager may have very different interests. The landlord wants the property to yield a maximum amount of profits with a minimal amount of trouble, but the manager's major concern is probably doing as little work as possible for his free rent. In this sort of situation you may be able to deal directly with the landlord with good results. This is especially true if the premises are not being kept clean or in good repair or if the manager is impolite. In any case, where communications are sticky or broken down, you should consider sending duplicate copies of letters and other communications to the landlord as well as to the manager.

Finding Out the Name of Your Landlord. In the past, some landlords have instructed their managers not to tell the tenants who they were or where they could be located, so the tenant could not "bother" them. A new law which applies only to buildings with more than two dwelling units tries to solve this problem. California Civil Code §1962 now provides that:

1. The rental agreement must state the name and address of both the manager and owner (or person authorized by him to receive notices, demands and law suits against the owner). This in-

---

*Usually a rental management corporation manages a lot of units in a relatively small geographic area. This makes checking their reputation fairly easy. It is wise to do so.

formation must be kept current with the tenant being informed of all changes,

OR,

2. Instead of putting this information in each rental agreement the landlord may choose to post notices containing the same information in the building. A notice must be posted in two easy to see places including elevators if they exist.

If the landlord fails to follow this law, then the person who rented the dwelling for the landlord automatically becomes his agent for receiving notices, demands and law suits.

B. THE LANDLORD BUSINESS

You may choose not to read this section and still learn all you need to know about what you face as a tenant. For those who are interested, however, we thought it would be helpful to understand how the landlord business works. We believe that a tenant or group of tenants will be in a better position to make wise decisions if they have an idea of what it's like to walk a mile in their landlord's boots.

Making money as a landlord depends a great deal on making wise initial investment decisions and on having an ability to manage property. This is true whether the landlord owns one unit or a thousand units. Given average ability in these directions, however, it is pretty difficult to lose money in the landlord business. Indeed, many landlords achieve spectacular returns. This is possible because the landlord is able to take advantage of a number of favorable tax laws and is able to use **your money** to do it.

The landlord business works something like this. To buy a building or building complex the landlord must usually put down between 10% and 25% of the purchase price. A bank or insurance company puts up the rest. If he buys a decent building he is then able to set the rents at a level that will allow him to cover all of his mortgage, tax and upkeep payments and pocket a little money besides. If you ask a landlord about his yearly profit he will doubt-less tell you that it is small, but will not tell you that each year he owns more of the building and in addition is receiving large tax deductions on his personal tax returns.

You have probably heard about "tax shelters" and "tax loop-holes." There are many of these available to landlords. Here is how tax laws work to benefit landlords:

- All the money a landlord pays for building maintenance and upkeep expense is subtracted from the landlord's profit figure before taxes are paid;

- All the money that a landlord pays in the form of interest on his mortgage payments constitutes a tax deduction. In the early years of a mortgage, interest will run as high as 80% to 90% of each payment;

- All the money a landlord pays in local property taxes constitutes a tax deduction;

- A percentage of the value of a landlord's buildings is deductible each year under the heading of "depreciation." The depreciation deduction allows the landlord credit for wear and tear to his building and the fact that the building is supposed to get less valuable as it gets older. If a landlord claims that a particular building has a useful life of 20 years, he is able to deduct 5% of the building's value each year. In some situations, a landlord is able to take advantage of laws that allow him to take extra depreciation in the early years of a mortgage. The depreciation deduction is often a major windfall for a landlord. This is because in most cases a building is more valuable after 20 years than it was when first purchased. Thus, the landlord gets his yearly tax deduction and a more valuable building too. As soon as the depreciation credits are used up, the wisdom of the landlord business dictates that the building be sold to a new landlord who then declares a new life expectancy for the building and starts the depreciation process all over again.

So far we have seen that a landlord has bought a building with a little bit of his own money and a lot of borrowed money. He then collects rent from you and other tenants, then uses your rent money to pay off his loan (mostly interest in the first years) and to pay property taxes and upkeep. With the exception of the small amount of money that represents the principal portion of each mortgage payment, he can deduct everything else from his taxes. Of course, the richer he is to start with, the more valuable the tax deductions become. Is it any wonder that the rich can't afford not to buy property?

15

There are still more reasons why the landlord business is so profitable. Unlike income that you pay taxes on at ordinary rates, your landlord is able to treat any profit he makes from selling rental property as "capital gains." This means that he is taxed at a rate of half of normal up to a **maximum** of 35% of his profit. Even if a person were to make many millions of dollars from the sale of an apartment complex, he would only pay taxes at a 35% rate. Landlords also get certain built-in advantages in times of inflation such as we are in now. A landlord benefits in that he is able to raise rental incomes while his mortgage and interest payments remain constant. In a similar way, the landlord often gets a break on his real property taxes. Normally a building is assessed for local property tax purposes on the basis of the original purchase price. In periods of inflation, however, rental income often goes up faster than do tax assessments.

With so much in the landlord's favor it is truly amazing that so many landlords are in unfavorable financial situations. When such is the case, it always goes hard on the tenants. If the landlord is foolish or greedy, he may get over extended on his loans (that is, if he may try to buy too much property without enough money, or if he may over-pay) then he will have to raise rents and/or cut back on repairs and services. This can lead to a high turn-over of dissatisfied or resentful tenants. Such circumstances can make the landlord harder to deal with, almost desperate.

Ask your landlord about his finances and problems. He'll appreciate your interest (making for an easier relationship), and you may learn something.

Landlords can be hurt quickly: (a) by periods of deflation and depression (the 1930's was a bad time for landlords) when they can't fill up their buildings with tenants at favorable rents; and (b) by any action by tenants to jointly withhold rents. None of these conditions has been widespread in California in recent years. As a result landlords have done very well and in many cases have made enormous profits. To see that these profits keep coming, landlords have organized at the local, state and federal levels. Through real estate associations, apartment house owners associations and similar groups, landlords keep a close watch on everything from your local city council and planning commission to the state and federal legislatures. Lobbyists maintain offices in Sacramento and Washington with the specific purpose of furthering the landlord business and seeing to it that no law harmful to landlords is passed by any legislature anywhere. Landlord lobbyists are also very successful at getting legislation introduced and enacted that is favorable to landlords.

C. LAWYERS

This book is not designed to replace an attorney. It is meant to help you decide whether or not you **need** one. The law says that you have a right to have an attorney represent you if you want one; no law says that you must have one.

The lawyer is an expert with words. His special talent is knowing what to say, who to say it to, and when to say it. If you always knew what to say, who to say it to, and when to say it, you wouldn't need a lawyer! The lawyer has special knowledge and special experience to help you make decisions. If you have sufficient information and knowledge available to you to make your own decisions, there may be no need for a lawyer.

Lawyers are in business to make money. They have to pay a lot of office overhead as well as support themselves and their families in a style to which they are, or would like to be, accustomed. Thus, most charge fairly high fees, normally in a range of $35 to $50 an hour. Clearly, when you have a dispute with your landlord which involves a few hundred dollars, it does not make good sense to pay someone as much, or more, to try to vindicate your position. In addition, there is always the danger that you will lose and end up paying both your landlord and your attorney, too.

This book is designed to give you a clear understanding of your rights and obligations. Hopefully by gaining such an understanding before getting into a dispute, the dispute can be avoided. This will not always be so, however, and disputes will occur where some kind of legal service is indicated.

1. WHAT LAWYERS CAN DO FOR YOU

There are three basic ways a lawyer can help with the kinds of problems that face a tenant:

a. Consultation and Advice

The lawyer can listen to the details of your situation, analyze it for you, and advise you on your position and best plan of action. Ideally he will give you more than just conclusions—he can educate you about your whole situation and tell you all the various alternatives available, then you can make your own choices. This kind of service is the least expensive as it only involves an office call and a little time. A charge of more than $25 to $35 for a consultation might be considered excessive. Find out the fee before you go in.

b. Negotiation

The lawyer can use his special talents, knowledge and experience to help you negotiate with the landlord to your best advantage. In case of serious problems, he can do this more successfully than you, especially if you are at odds with the landlord, or if your landlord has an attorney. Without spending much of his own time, he can often accomplish a lot through a letter or phone call. Receiving a message on an attorney's letterhead is, in itself, often very sobering to a landlord. He knows you mean business! A lawyer can sometimes possess considerable skill as a negotiator. Also, if bad turns to worse, a lawyer can often bluff by threatening legal action. You can then decide at a later time whether to actually pursue it.

c. Law Suits

In some rare instances your case may merit going into court with a law suit. Having your lawyer go into court is very expensive, and only rarely warranted. If the landlord sues you first, it is a little more likely that you will end up in court, and very likely that you will need a lawyer's help.

Whenever you think of using a lawyer, keep in mind this view of clients that is held by a lawyer-friend of ours: he imagines a man who has built a shack on some old railroad tracks in a high mountain valley. One day, when he puts his ear to the track, the man hears a distant vibration. A few days later he can hear the sound of a train rumbling on the warm breeze that blows up the canyon, and soon the sound is distinctly audible. At this point he can begin to see the smoke of the engine, and not much later the train is running down on him, spitting fire and belching smoke. When the thing is fifty yards away, he picks up his phone, calls his lawyer and asks him to get an injunction against the railroad company! What we mean to say is . . . if you decide to use a lawyer, don't wait until it's too late.

2. WHEN DO YOU NEED A LAWYER?

There is no simple answer to the question of when you need a lawyer. This is because there are many possible areas of dispute between landlord and tenant, and many levels of tenant ability to deal with problems. Throughout this book we will suggest times when the advice or other services of an attorney would be useful, but here are a few general pointers:

a. If you have a lease or a written rental agreement which allows attorney fees for your landlord, then California law says that the tenant is also entitled to recover attorney fees if he wins a law suit based on the terms of that agreement;

b. If your landlord sues you for a lot of money, see an attorney;

c. If you have any problem that you can't understand or solve by reading this book, you should try to get some professional advice.

3. FINDING A LAWYER

Finding a lawyer who charges reasonable prices and whom you feel can be trusted is not always an easy task. There is always the fear that by just picking a name out of the telephone book you may get someone unsympathetic (perhaps an attorney who specializes in representing landlords) or an attorney who will charge too much. You should realize that these are common fears and that you are not the only one who feels a little scared and intimidated. Here are some suggestions:

a. Legal Aid

If you are **very** poor, you may qualify for free help from your Legal Aid office. Check your phone directory for their location, or ask your County Clerk.

b. Group Legal Practices

A new but rapidly growing aspect of California law practice is the Group Legal Practice program. Many groups, including unions, employers and consumer action groups, are offering plans to their members whereby they can get legal assistance for rates which are substantially lower than offered by most private practitioners. Some of these plans are good, some mediocre, and a few are not worth it, but most are better than nothing. In the San Francisco Bay region, a good plan is offered through the Consumers' Cooperative of Berkeley at 1414 University Avenue, Berkeley. Because the group practices area of the law is changing so rapidly, we can't give you a statewide list of group legal plans. If you contact the above group, however, they may be able to help you find a good group practice plan in your area.

c. Private Attorneys

If you don't know an attorney that can be trusted and can't get a reliable recommendation from a friend, you have a problem. While you might be lucky and randomly pick an attorney who matches your needs perfectly, you might just as easily wind up paying too much for too little. Here are some suggestions that should make your search a little easier:

- Lawyers can now legally advertise. Check the yellow pages and other media for people who say they specialize in tenant problems. Organizations calling themselves "Legal Clinics" often provide help to tenants at a more reasonable price than do regular law firms.

- Avoid referral panels set up by local bar associations. Any

21

lawyer can get on these panels by paying a fee. You would do as well, and often better, to stick a pin in the attorneys section of the phone book. Also, sticking a pin in the phone book is free whereas some of the reference panel systems will charge you as much as $25 for the referral;

- Check with a local consumer organization to see if they can recommend someone;

- Shop around by calling different law offices and stating your problem. Ask them how much it would cost for a visit. Try to talk to a lawyer personally to attempt to get an idea of how friendly and sympathetic he is to your concerns;

- Remember, lawyers whose offices and life styles are reasonably simple are more likely to help you for less money than lawyers who feel naked unless wearing a $300 outfit. You should be able to find an attorney willing to discuss your problems for $15 to $35.

D. RENTERS' TAX CREDIT— CALIFORNIA INCOME TAX

California allows a tax credit of $37 to people who rent their principal dwelling place and who are not claimed as a dependent by another taxpayer.* If you pay taxes, you subtract the credit from the amount owed. If you don't pay taxes, you can still get the credit. This means you file a return and the state pays you. Married couples can only get one credit, but people living together can each claim one. In addition, tenants 62 years of age or older and whose annual income is $5,000 or less are eligible for tax benefits due to the fact that part of their rent is used to pay property taxes.** For technical details on these benefits, see the Individual Income Tax Guide put out by the California Franchise Tax Board.

*Revenue and Taxation Code section 17053.5
**Revenue and Taxation Code section 19523.5

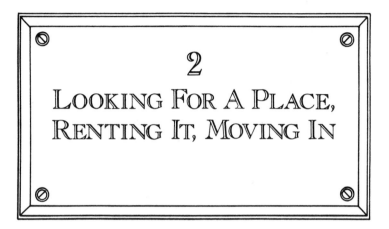

2
LOOKING FOR A PLACE, RENTING IT, MOVING IN

A. GET ORGANIZED

Looking for a house or apartment to rent is often a frustrating and time-consuming task. Since it is human nature to get harried and frazzled under pressure, many mistakes are made at this stage which later turn out to be costly, both in time and money.* Try to stay cool.

Before you start looking for a place, decide how much you want to pay, how long you plan on staying and what sort of area you want to live in. Be realistic both as to your own budget and as to what is available, and set definite guidelines in advance. If you find a place that fits your needs right away you should celebrate. But if you can't find a place that meets your guidelines, under no circumstances change them without taking time to think the matter over carefully. Some of the worst and most costly mistakes are made by people who sign a lease or put down a deposit at the end of a long frustrating day only to realize later that the place is completely unsuitable.

---

*Be wary of companies that claim to be "homefinding services," or run ads, listing what seem to be exceedingly desirable properties at low rents. Certainly many "homefinding services" are on the level, but the S. F. Bay Guardian, after an investigation, found in their October 4, 1974 issue that a surprising number are rip-offs. .Do a little investigating before you pay anyone to find a home for you.

It is extremely important that you keep all records. As a part of your getting organized, get a large manilla envelope or file folder in which to keep all papers having to do with your rental transaction. Misplacing and losing papers (deposit agreements, leases, rent receipts, etc.) is a common mistake that should be avoided. Your landlord is in business and has probably learned how not to make such basic mistakes, so you should do the same. Set up a safe place in which to save your papers and anything else that you think might possibly be important at a later time.

B. LEARN ABOUT RENTAL AGREEMENTS

Before you start looking for a place, you should know a little about rental agreements.

NUMBER ONE RULE: Don't sign any papers until you understand what's in them, or you may regret it later. Reading these next few sections should help you to such an understanding, for, after all, there are only three different kinds of rental agreements, and all you really need to know is what they are like and the consequences to you of the different ones. If you know these few things you may be able to bargain for better terms, and you'll know better when to turn down an agreement altogether. If you read this chapter and still don't understand what's in your agreement, you should probably get some advice (see Chapter 1, Part C) before you make the deal.

1. THE THREE KINDS OF RENTAL AGREEMENTS

There are just three basic ways that residential rentals are commonly made: the Lease, the Written Rental Agreement and the Oral Rental Agreement. An oral agreement is made without anything being written down—you just speak out what the deal is and agree to it. The other two, the Lease and the Written Rental Agreement, have all the terms you agree to written down on a paper which you and the landlord sign.

2. ORAL AGREEMENTS

It is perfectly legal to make a deal orally—that is, without writing anything down, and no signatures. The landlord agrees to let you move in and you agree to pay rent on some schedule, like weekly, every other week or every month. The period between rent payments is what determines how much notice you are entitled to for rent raises or orders to get out. If you pay (a) weekly or (b) monthly, then you are entitled to (a) a week's or (b) 30 days notice.

The Oral Agreement has some advantages, in that it is relatively informal, you can move out on short notice, and you aren't subjected to the long list of terms and rules contained in most Leases and Written Rental Contracts. However, if you want the clarity of having everything written down, you may want your deal in writing, and if you want long-term security from rent raises and orders to move out, you will want a lease.

Oral agreements are legal, enforceable and have some advantages. But as time goes by and circumstances change, people's memories can have a funny habit of changing, too. Then, if something goes wrong, both sides end up in front of a judge who has to decide whom to believe. For this reason, even if you take an oral agreement, it may become very important to have some of the landlord's promises in writing. Therefore, if he promises to make repairs, return security deposits, or if he makes any other kind of deal with you that you want to make sure he remembers, then just ask him to write it down, date and sign it.

3. LEASES AND WRITTEN RENTAL AGREEMENTS

The Lease and the Written Rental Agreement are basically the same except for one terribly important difference:

THE LEASE fixes all the terms of the agreement so that no changes can be made for a given period of time—most commonly, one year. If you rent under a Lease, your rent cannot be raised until the Lease runs out nor can you be told to move unless you break the terms of the Lease. On the other hand, **you** can't easily get out of your obligations under the Lease until it runs out.

THE WRITTEN RENTAL AGREEMENT has everything written down, just like the Lease, but the time period is either indefinite, or else short—usually 30 days. This means that you can move out or your landlord can raise your rent or order you to move out on only 30 days' notice (sometimes less).

Except for these very important differences, Leases and Written Rental Agreements are so much alike that they are sometimes hard to tell apart if you're not careful. Both of them cover the basic terms of the rental (names, addresses, amount of rent and date due, deposits, etc.) and both of them tend to have a lot of other fine print provisions to protect the landlord. When they are printed, they look alike, and the title at the top of the document can be misleading.

Legally, a written agreement can be typed or written down in longhand on any kind of paper, in any words, so long as the terms are understandable. However, as a practical matter, nearly all landlords use standard printed forms which they buy in stationery stores or get from landlord associations. These forms have been prepared by lawyers or real estate associations, and they are as favorable as possible to the landlord. These forms need not look like a death certificate, nor read like an act of Congress, but such is often the case. Some of the worst ones include paragraphs by which you sign away your privacy, accept shorter than normal notice periods for rent increases and termination, accept responsibility for fixing things that should be handled by your landlord and generally elevate the landlord into the position of a minor dictator. In the next section we discuss the common provisions and tell you some things to watch out for.

You will find a lease and rental agreement form fair to both landlord and tenant at the back of this book (see also section 6 on page 34).

BE CAREFUL! Since they look so much alike, some forms can look like a lease, and sound like a lease, and even cover a year's period, but if they contain a provision that rent can be raised or that the agreement can be terminated on 30 days notice, then they are really only Written Rental Agreements.

READ IT CAREFULLY! It is **crucial** that you read the entire Lease and understand it before you sign it. If the Lease refers to another document such as "house rules" make sure you read a copy of these too. If there is any part of the written document that you don't understand, get advice (but not from the people who want you to sign the lease). If you want your rights protected, you will have to see to it yourself.

If the Lease offered to you by the prospective landlord is not satisfactory, it is legal and simple to change it if both parties can agree on the changes. All you do is cross out unwanted portions, write in desired changes, and have all parties who are going to sign the document initial the changes.

ORAL PROMISES MAY NOT BE WORTH THE AIR IT TAKES TO MAKE THEM. Whenever there is a written agreement the law presumes that the parties wrote down **all** of the parts to it before they signed it. If the landlord makes promises which aren't written down, it is assumed they weren't made. Get everything you want included in writing before you sign.

4. COMMON PROVISIONS IN PRINTED FORMS AND WHAT TO WATCH OUT FOR

This section is about the fine print on the form agreements. There are probably hundreds of different printed forms and the provisions in them are all worded a little differently. It is often not at all obvious what some provisions mean (contrary to what form writers seem to think, it is **not** illegal to use plain English and be clear). We try to simplify the whole problem for you by setting out, in the list below, the most common kinds of printed form provisions, together with what they usually mean, and what to watch out for.

As will be seen, some of the provisions are illegal and therefore unenforceable. How to bargain with the landlord about them is no problem—since they are worthless, you should probably not waste your bargaining power by trying to get the landlord to scratch them out. It may sometimes help, however, to mention to him that these provisions are illegal, in order to show him how one-sided the agreement is, and then ask him to eliminate or change other (enforceable) provisions. There are some provisions which may be damaging to you later, so we advise you to try to get them out.

Whether you want to use your bargaining power on lease

changes, however, rather than on trying to get repairs or a lower rent or lower security deposit, is a judgment you will have to make.

Many printed forms contain the following kinds of provisions:

a. Provision Against Assignment or Sub-lease Without Landlord's Consent

This prevents you from getting out of a lease by finding another tenant to take your place. You may want to try to get it scratched out or at least changed to state that the landlord cannot reject any new tenant that you find to replace you unless his credit or behavior is bad. (see Chapter 7).

b. Provision that the Landlord is not Responsible for Damage

This provision says that if the landlord is negligent in maintaining the place and you, your family, or your property is injured (for example, by falling down broken stairs), the landlord is not responsible for paying for your losses. This is called an "exculpatory" provision. Under a new statute (Civil Code section 1953, effective Janauary 1, 1975), such a provision is invalid.

c. Waiver or Tenant's Rights under Civil Code Sections 1941 and 1942; or Making Tenant Responsible for Repairs

This provision requires the tenant to waive his rights under Civil Code Sections 1941 and 1942 to make repairs himself and deduct the cost from his rent. This waiver is not valid, so don't use up your bargaining power by making an issue of it.

The agreement might instead contain a provision requiring **you** to repair or maintain the premises. This provision does not relieve the landlord of his obligation **to the State** to see that the place complies with the housing codes. It might, however, stop you from exercising any rights **you** have (to repair and deduct, for example) against the landlord if he fails to make repairs. Therefore, try to get such a provision scratched out. Tell the landlord that the law imposes an obligation on **him** to make the place livable, and he should not try to pass this off on his tenants.

d. Waiver of Right to Legal Notice

This provision says the landlord can sue to evict you or can raise the rent or change the terms of the lease without giving any notice (such as a three day notice to pay your rent or vacate) required by law. It is not valid. (Civil Code Section 1953).

e. Provision Setting Notice Period

This provision sets the amount of time the landlord must give you before his notice of termination or rent raise or change in terms becomes operative. If there is no such provision, and you are a month-to-month tenant, the law requires that he give you 30 days notice. The law permits, however, such a provision to cut the notice period **down** to as low as **seven** days. This is very bad for you. If there is such a provision in the agreement, try to get it scratched out. Tell the landlord that you will need at least 30 days to find another place if he decides to terminate your tenancy or raise your rent.

f. Right to Inspect

Many forms have a provision which gives the landlord the right to come into your place to inspect it, or for other purposes.

Under a new statute, the landlord's right to enter the dwelling is limited to certain reasons, and any attempt to add to these reasons in the lease or rental agreement is void. See page 64.

g. "Right of Re-entry" Provision

This provision permits the landlord to come in and throw you out if you don't pay the rent, without giving you legal notice of going to court. It is not valid.

h. Waiver of Jury Trial

This provision says that you waive your right to a trial by jury in any eviction law suit brought by the landlord. It is not valid.

i. Waiver of Right to Appeal

This provision prevents you from appealing a court decision in any eviction law suit. It is not valid.

j. Treble Damages

This provision says that if the landlord sues to evict you and wins, he may get not just the actual damages he has suffered (usually unpaid rent), but three times as much. The law provides for something very much like this anyway, so you might as well leave this provision alone.

k. Landlord's Attorney's Fees

This provision says that if the landlord has to sue to evict you or collect rent, you will pay his attorney's fees. This can amount to $150 to $200 or more. This provision is valid, and the landlord cannot get attorney's fees unless he has such a provision. Therefore, try to get it scratched out. If you lose your job or your welfare is cut off and you can't pay the rent, you don't want a judgment against you for attorney's fees in addition to back rent. (When you later get a job, the landlord can have this money taken out of your paycheck.)

Whenever you have such a provision, the law says that the attorney's fee provision entitles **you** to collect **your** attorney's fees from the landlord if you win the eviction law suit, even if the provision does not say this.

l. Late Charges

This provision requires the tenant to pay a late charge if he pays his rent late. The charge may be a percentage of the rent (such as 4%) or a flat fee (such as $5.00). This provision might be valid.* Try to get it scratched out, or at least have the landlord write that it doesn't apply if you cannot pay your rent on time for some good reason, such as delay in getting your paycheck or welfare check.

m. Entire Agreement

Somewhere in the fine print, usually at the end, most leases have a provision which says that the agreement is the **entire** agreement of the parties. That means that if

---

*Some recent cases indicate that late charge provisions might be successfully challenged. **Gar-rett** v. **South Coast Fed. S. I. L.,** 9 Cal. 3d 731 (1973); **Clermont** v. **Secured Investment Corp.,** 25 Cal. App. 3d 766 (1972); **Kirby** v. **Mann,** (San Mateo Muni, Ct., 1973) 78 Clearinghouse Review 685.

the landlord made any promises which weren't written down, then they don't count and can't be enforced. It pays, under all circumstances, to get all promises from the landlord in writing.

5. WHICH IS BETTER, A LEASE OR RENTAL AGREEMENT?

If you have a lease for a substantial term, like a year, you are assured that the landlord cannot evict you or raise the rent so long as you pay your rent on time and meet your other obligations under the lease. This kind of security is good to have if housing is hard to find and rents are rising, which is the situation in many California communities.

On the other hand, a lease also locks **you** in for the term. You can't easily move out to take a better place or get lower rent, as you could do if you had a month-to-month rental agreement merely by giving 30 days notice. If you have a lease and move out before the term is up, the landlord could sue you for the rent as it comes due until the lease runs out or until he finds another tenant, whichever comes first. If the lease allows you to find another tenant and sublease, of course, you might avoid this problem, but even then you will have to pay the rent if the subtenant doesn't pay. Chapter 7, Part C, tells you how to break a lease if you have to, but even so, it is a lot of trouble.

All things being equal, if there is a good chance you will want to move before the term of a lease is up, you should probably have a month-to-month rental agreement rather than a lease.

The written rental agreement is often preferred by landlords. It gives them the right to raise the rent as often as they wish, to get rid of tenants that they don't like and insert all sorts of clauses telling the tenant what he can't do. In most cases, from a tenant's point of view, the written rental agreement does not have the advantages of either a lease or an oral agreement.

On the other hand, you often have to take what you can get. We did. At this writing, two of the authors live (happily) under written rental agreements. No choice.

6. MODEL LEASE AND MODEL RENTAL AGREEMENT

Most landlords' forms are very unfair. They impose many requirements on the tenant and very few on the landlord. We offer a positive alternative for you to use, if you get the chance. Included at page 184 are copies of two tear-out forms which are fair to both parties. They require the tenant to pay his rent and keep up his apartment while requiring the landlord to make repairs and not hassle the tenant. They leave out the harsh provisions found in most landlords' leases. Try to get your landlord to agree to use one of these forms instead of his. Read the sections above to help you decide whether you want to use the Lease or the Rental Agreement.

Additional printed copies of the tear-out forms can be obtained by writing to the Nolo Press, P. O. Box 544, Occidental, California 95465. Please include 80c for each form (5 for $2.50) and be sure to specify whether you want the lease or rental agreement.

C. SECURITY DEPOSITS, CLEANING FEES AND LAST MONTH'S RENT

Landlords usually require some type of deposit when they make a deal with a tenant. The landlord might call this deposit a "security deposit," "cleaning fee," or "last month's rent." Many tenants listen to such a label, do not really understand it, and then when they want to move out they don't know if they have a right to get the money back.

To avoid headaches later, you and the landlord must clearly understand at the outset what the deposit is for and when you can get it back. Once you reach this understanding, make sure to get it in writing, either as part of the rental document or in its own.

1. SECURITY DEPOSIT

When a landlord asks for a "security deposit," he usually wants some money to hold as security from loss of rent or damage to his property. If he requires you to clean the place before you leave, he wants security for costs of cleaning too. If you leave without paying rent or paying for breakage or cleaning the place properly, the landlord doesn't want to be bothered with finding you and suing you. He will just keep all or part of your security deposit.

Effective for all leases and oral and written rental agreements created or renewed on or after January 1, 1978 on residential property, the landlord is limited to collecting deposits or fees for cleaning when you leave, repair and non-payment of rent in an amount no greater than two months' rent if the property is unfurnished, and three months' rent if it is furnished. These amounts are in addition to any rent paid for the first month of occupancy, but include last month's rent paid in advance. Cal. Civil Code Section 1950.5.

As just noted the total amount that a landlord can charge for all types of deposits and fees is two times one month's rent if the place is unfurnished and three times if it is furnished. This means that if the rent is $300 per month and the apartment is not furnished, the landlord can charge up to a total of $600 for deposits and last month's rent.

When you move out, if you don't owe any rent, haven't broken anything, and have properly cleaned the place, the landlord must return your security deposit. If you do owe him something, he can keep what you owe him but must give you an itemized written statement as to what was retained and why and return the balance of your deposit. He must return whatever you have coming and give you the itemized statement within two weeks after you leave. If he refuses to return what you have coming, you can sue him to get it back. If you can also show that his refusal to return it was not because of some honest dispute but because he just wanted to cheat you, you might be able to collect "punitive damages" of up to $200 against him.*

In parts F and G below, we tell you some steps to take when you move in to make sure you get your deposit back, and, in Chapter 8, Part B, we discuss what to do when you move out to get your deposits back, and how to handle trouble at that time.**

Cleaning deposits are just that, deposits that must be returned to the tenant when he or she moves out and leaves the place clean. Like security deposits, cleaning deposits are regulated

---

*Civil Code Section 1950.5. See Chapter 8, Part B.

Some landlords have begun using companies which offer the landlord "protection" from bad tenants. Here's how it usually works: The landlord tells the tenant to see the company if the tenant doesn't want to put up the security deposit. The tenant pays the company a credit-check fee (about $7) **and, if the tenant's credit is OK, a "protection fee" of about 15% of the security deposit. None of this is refundable, and note that if the tenant damages the premises, he **still** must pay for the damage (and cannot apply the "protection fee" to the cost of repairing the damage). This doesn't look like a very good deal for the tenant, to us.

under Section 1950.5 of the Civil Code. As noted above, a landlord can charge deposits (in addition to first month's rent, but including last month's rent) in an amount equal to twice one month's rent if a place is unfurnished, and three times one month's rent if it is furnished. This includes deposits and fees for cleaning, security and last month's rent. Thus, if a landlord charges you a $300 "security deposit" on an unfurnished flat that rents for $300 per month, he or she can charge an additional $300 for a "cleaning deposit".

But what about "fees" which the landlord claims to be "non-refundable"? For all tenancies commenced or renewed after January 1, 1978 (this includes all month-to-month tenancies), non-refundable fees are no longer legal except for very specific purposes which we discuss below. This means that, generally speaking, all fees and charges for cleaning and security are refundable and that, if they are not returned within two weeks (unless the landlord has a valid reason for their retention) of your moving out, you can sue to get them back and may be able to recover an additional $200 in punitive damages.

There is one exception to this rule. It is set out in subsection (c) of 1950.5 and says: "This subdivision shall not be construed to preclude a landlord and a tenant from entering into a mutual agreement for the landlord, at the request of the tenant and for a specified fee or charge, to make structural, decorative, furnishing or other similar alterations." The intent of this clause is clearly to compensate the landlord for strange or unusual alterations requested by the tenant, but there is a danger that some landlords may try to re-introduce "cleaning" or "security" type fees under it. Be awake to this possibility!

3. LAST MONTH'S RENT *

Some landlords will ask that you pay the "last month's rent" in advance. This means just what it says—if you have a year's lease from January 1 to December 31, by paying "last month's rent" you are paying the rent for December in advance. If you have a month-to month rental agreement, when you give notice that you are leaving in 30 days, your "last month's rent" will take care of your last month.

Landlords want "last month's rent" so that if you fail to pay

---

*Section 1950.5 now states that effective for all tenancies commenced or renewed after January 1, 1978, all deposits taken together (including those for last month's rent) are limited to twice the monthly rental amount for unfurnished units and three times the monthly rental amount for furnished units.

your rent some month, they can treat that as the last month, evict you, and not lose any rent for that month.

The landlord **cannot** use the "last month's rent" as a security deposit for damage to the place. If he wants to collect for that sort of thing, he will have to sue you. Thus it is generally better for the tenant to pay "last month's rent" than a security deposit. (Best, of course, is paying none of these.)

If the tenant gives a security deposit and not last month's rent, he will have to pay the last month's rent when it comes due and then the **tenant** has to worry about how to get the security deposit back when he moves out. If the tenant pays only "last month's rent" in advance, the **landlord** has to worry about getting money from the tenant for any damages he claims. It's much better to have your money and let the other guy figure out how to get it, rather than the other way around.

4. "HOLDING" DEPOSIT

Sometimes if you make a deal with a landlord he will want some type of cash deposit, then and there, to make sure you don't change your mind and back out of the deal. If you give him the cash, usually around $20, he will "hold" the place for you until you bring him your first month's rent and any deposits or fees you agreed on. This is called a "holding" or "bond" deposit.

If you give him a holding deposit and later decide not to take the place, you probably will be unable to get your deposit back. Therefore, be sure you really want the place before giving this kind of deposit.

Be sure you and the landlord understand what is to happen to the deposit when you take the place. Usually it will be applied to the first month's rent. To make this clear, have the landlord give you a receipt for the deposit and have him write on the receipt what is to happen to the deposit when you come back with the rent.

5. CREDIT CHECK FEE

Landlords can, and often do, charge a non-refundable fee to check the credit of prospective tenants. Credit checks normally cost no more than $10-$15 and we believe that charging more than this is unreasonable. It is never wise to rent from an unreasonable landlord no matter how desirable the place.

D. HOW TO CHECK A PLACE OVER BEFORE YOU RENT IT

If you see a place that you think you will like, take a walk around the neighborhood. Check out where there are stores, schools and bus stops. Walk around the building you are interested in renting and try to meet some of the neighbors. Ask them how they have gotten along with the landlord. Make sure that you can feel at home in all respects. Take an especially close look at the condition of the unit you may rent. Look for dirt and damage, and carefully check all doors, windows, screens, stoves, furnaces, hot water heaters and any other appliances. Make lists of any defects you find—later you can negotiate with the landlord for improvements and repairs. At the very least, be sure to get him to sign an acknowledgment of the existing conditions, so he can't blame you later for causing them.

In the section below we cover the landlord's responsibilities for the condition of the premises he rents. Then we show you exactly how to carefully check a place out to see if it meets legal standards.

1. HOUSING CODES AND ENFORCEMENT

Housing codes are laws which require a landlord to put his apartments and houses in good condition before renting them and to keep them that way while people are living there. The landlord cannot escape this duty by trying to impose it on the tenant in the lease or rental agreement.

California has a State Housing Law. The main part of this law is contained in a little brown book called Uniform Building Code, Vol. III, Housing (1973 Edition). You can get a copy by sending a check or money order for $3.41 to International Conference of Building Officials, 5360 South Workman Mill Road, Whittier, California 90601. Violation of the State Housing Law is a crime, punishable by a fine of up to $500 or imprisonment for up to six months, or both.*

Many cities and counties have also enacted housing codes. Local rules are at least as strict as the State Housing Law. Check with your City Clerk and County Clerk to see if you have such laws in your community.

The State Housing Law and local housing codes are enforced by local agencies. These are usually city and county Building Inspection Departments. Other local agencies which might help you with certain health and housing conditions are the Health Department and Fire Department.

If you call a local agency such as a Building Inspection Department and tell them that your landlord won't make repairs, they will send out a building inspector. He will carefully inspect the place and make a report. If he finds housing code violations, he will send a letter to the landlord ordering him to make repairs. If

---

*Health and Safety Code Section 17995.

he does not make them within a reasonable time, the inspector may order the building vacated until repairs are made, order the building demolished, or have the work done and charge the cost to the landlord.

In addition, **you** may be able to "enforce" the codes by suing the landlord, using rent money to make repairs, or withholding rent. These remedies are discussed in Chapter 6.

2. A CHECKLIST OF THINGS TO INSPECT

Here is a checklist of things you should look for when inspecting a place. All requirements mentioned are contained in the State Housing Law.

a. Check the STRUCTURE (floors, walls, ceiling, foundation).

The structure of the place must be weatherproof, water-proof and rodent proof.

"Weatherproof" means there must be no holes, cracks, or broken plaster. Check to see if all the walls are flush (that they meet directly, with no space in between). See if any floorboards are warped. Does wall plaster fall off when you touch it?

"Waterproof" means no water should leak in. If you see dark round spots on the ceilings or dark streaks on the walls, rain water might have been leaking through.

"Rodent proof" deals with cracks and holes which rats and mice could use.

b. Check the PLUMBING.

The landlord does not have to provide you with water, but he must provide a plumbing system connected to your community's water system and also to its sewage system (unless you have a cesspool).

All plumbing must be in a good condition, free of rust and leaks. Sometimes the condition of the plumbing is hard to discover, but there are several tests you can run to see if there might be problems.

Flush the toilet. Does it take too long to flush? Does it leak on the floor? Is the water discolored? If so, the pipes may be rusty or unclean.

If the water is connected, fill a sink with hot and cold water. Turn the faucets on all the way, and listen for vibrating or knocking sounds in the pipes. See if the water in the sink is discolored. Drain the sink, and see if it takes too long for the water to run out.

c. Check the BATHROOM.

The State and Housing Law requires that every apartment and house have at least one working toilet, wash basin, and bathtub (or shower) in it. The toilet and bathtub (or shower) must be in a room which gives privacy to the occupant and which is ventilated. All of these facilities must be installed and maintained in a safe and sanitary condition.

d. Check the KITCHEN.

The State Housing Law requires that every apartment and house have a kitchen. The kitchen must have a kitchen sink, which cannot be made of wood or other absorbent material.

e. Check the HOT WATER.

The landlord must see that you have both hot and cold running water (although he can require you to pay the water and gas bills). "Hot" water means a temperature of not less than 120 degrees F.

f. Check the HEAT.

The landlord must provide heating facilities which can maintain a temperature of 70 degrees F. at a point three feet above the floor in all rooms you live in. Unvented fuel-burning heaters are not permitted.

g. Check the LIGHT AND VENTILATION.

All rooms you live in must have natural light through windows or skylights, which must have an area not less than one-tenth of the floor area of the room, with a minimum of 12 square feet (3 square feet for bathroom windows). The windows must be openable at least half way for ventilation, unless mechanical ventilation is provided.

Hallways and stairs in the building must be lighted at all times.

h. Check for signs of INSECTS, VERMIN AND RODENTS.

The landlord must provide facilities to prevent insect and rodent infestation and, if there is infestation, provide for extermination services.

These pests can be hard to notice. Remember, however, that they are very shy and stay out of sight. Therefore, if you see any fresh **signs** of them, they are probably very numerous and will bother you later on. Also, these pests travel from house to house. If your neighbors have them, they will probably get to you.

Check for rodent trails and excrement. Rats and mice travel the same path day after day and leave a gray coloring along the floor and baseboards. Look at the kitchen carefully, for rodents go there for food supplies. Check in closets, cupboards, and behind appliances for cockroaches.

Check for possible breeding grounds nearby. Stagnant water is often a source of pests. So are garages and basements that have piles of litter or old couches.

As mentioned before, cracks and holes in the walls and floors can be entry-points for pests.

i. Check the WIRING AND ELECTRICITY.

Loose or exposed wiring can be dangerous, leading to shock or fires. The landlord must provide safe and proper wiring.

If electrical power is available in the area, the place must be connected to it. Every room you live in must have at least two outlets (or one outlet and one light fixture). Every bathroom must have at least one light fixture.

j. Check for FIRE SAFETY.

The landlord must provide safe exits leading to a street or hallway. Hallways, stairways and exits must be free from litter. Storage rooms, garages, and basements must not contain combustible materials.

k. Check for adequate TRASH AND GARBAGE RECEPTACLES.

The landlord must provide adequate garbage and trash storage and removal facilities. Garbage cans must have tight-fitting covers.

l. Check the general CLEANLINESS OF THE AREA.

The landlord must keep those parts of the building which he controls (hallways, stairs, yards, basement, driveway, etc.) in a clean, sanitary, and safe condition.

3. WHAT IF THE PLACE DOES NOT MEET THE ABOVE STANDARDS?

If the place has serious problems, you should probably not rent it if you can possibly avoid it. A landlord who would even show you such a place probably won't or can't make the needed repairs. If the landlord promises to fix it up, be careful. First, ask other tenants how good the landlord is at keeping such promises. Second, make him put his promises in writing and sign it. Be sure he puts down **dates** on which certain repairs will be completed. Also, get him to write down that you will not have to pay your rent if he fails to meet the completion dates. If he doesn't want to agree to these things, he probably isn't taking his obligation to repair very seriously.

If you like the place but it has a few problems, simply ask the landlord to promise to make the necessary repairs. You might point out to him that he is required to do this before renting, under the State Housing Law, but you will rent the place and let him repair it later if he makes his promise (with dates) in writing and signs it.

If the landlord refuses to make the repairs, or if the place is so bad you don't trust his promises to make repairs, you should not rent the place, but you should report him to your city or county Building Inspection Department. He is violating the law (the State Housing Law), so this is your duty as a citizen. Also, you may be helping the tenant who ends up having to take the place.

E. HOW TO BARGAIN FOR THE BEST DEAL

Once you decide that you might like to rent a particular place you then negotiate the terms of the rental with the landlord or his agent. Often you will be presented with a "take it or leave it" proposition where the landlord is not open to making changes. Many times, however, landlords will be open to reasonable changes. Whether it be the rent that you are trying to change, or particular terms in the contract, it never hurts to try.

In your first negotiations it is good to remember that if the landlord is impressed with you he will be more likely to want you as a tenant. Take a moment to consider what sort of folks you would like to rent to if you were a landlord. In fact, you might think over the information in Chapter 1 about your landlord and his situation. Certainly, a good first impression can be made on the application form. Most landlords ask you to fill out an application listing your jobs, banks, cars, income and references. Be ready to make your application look as good as possible. Be coldly factual on information that the landlord can check easily and save exaggeration for those areas that can be checked only with difficulty.

How good a deal you can get from a landlord depends on how badly he wants you. If there are very few places available at the rent he is asking and a lot of people are looking, he may tell you to take his deal (rent, security deposit and form lease) or forget the whole thing. Even in such cases you may be able to squeeze a few concessions out of him which may save you money or hassles later on.

If there are lots of places for rent and not too many people looking, you will have more bargaining power. The landlord wants to rent the place soon (to get the rent) and may be afraid of losing you to another landlord.

Try to find out the situation before you bargain with a landlord. A good way is to see how long he has been trying to rent the place. Ask neighbors, or see how long he has had ads in the newspaper. If he has been trying for more than a month, he will be worried. If he has lowered the rent since he first started trying to rent it, he is really worried. Take advantage of it.

If you can, try to talk to the last tenant that lived in the place. He might give you some very valuable information about how to deal with the landlord, what is wrong with the place, and generally what it is like to live there. Other tenants or neighbors in the area might also be helpful on this.

The better you look as a responsible tenant, the more bargaining power you will have. Every landlord wants "responsible" tenants who will pay rent regularly, not mess up his place, and not complain about anything. The more you appear to be this way, the better the deal you will get. The landlord won't rent to you at all unless he trusts you, and if he trusts you, he may be willing to give you things you ask for in order to keep you.

If you have any bargaining power, try to use it. You are investing a lot of your money and energy for a long time to come, and you are entitled to shop around and bargain to get the best deal you can.

Some people don't like to bargain, because they think others will think they are cheap. But don't forget that the landlord is trying to get as much as he can out of his tenants, and he is not considered cheap, but a "good businessman." You should be a "good consumer" and get as much as you can for as little as you can get away with.

Even if the rent is fair and the landlord won't budge on that, there are other things he might give you if you ask. He may have a better refrigerator in storage or he may be willing to eliminate some lease provisions you don't like, or he may do some other things mentioned in this Handbook.

F. GET ALL PROMISES IN WRITING

Your future relationship with your landlord may be very pleasant. Hope for the best and try to be open, honest and friendly. However, at the same time, sensible steps should be taken for your own self protection just in case things take a nasty turn.

It often happens that a tenant moves into an apartment which has not been properly cleaned, or which needs painting or repairs. The landlord may say that the tenant can leave it in the same condition when he leaves, or perhaps that he can deduct money from the rent in exchange for cleaning, painting or repairs. Whatever promises the landlord makes, you should be aware that it is very common for this sort of vague, oral agreement to lead to misunderstanding, bitterness and financial loss. The time to protect yourself is at the beginning. This may be your only chance to do so.

If a landlord promises to clean, paint, make repairs, reimburse you for material and work, or if there are any other kinds of prom-

ises you want to depend upon, get them in writing and put a date for completing the work. Asking for a promise in writing need not cause you tension or embarassment. Just tell the landlord, politely, that you have made a simple list of what has been agreed to, and that you want to go over it with him for clarification. If he agrees that the list is accurate, have him date and sign it. There should be two copies, one for the landlord and one for your own files.

The use of contracts is standard among business people and among friends when they are in a business relationship. The purpose of such writings is to remind people of what they once agreed to do. If the landlord balks at putting things in writing, be very careful in all dealings with him.

Once the tenant moves in, it often takes landlords a long time to get around to doing promised work and if there is nothing in writing, sometimes the work never gets done. It is particularly important to get in writing any promise to reduce rent in exchange for material or your own labor. Every year thousands of landlords and tenants get into bitter disputes about this sort of agreement. It is not uncommon for the landlord's memory to get a little short after the work has been done.

If the landlord won't paint, clean or make repairs, be sure to list the faults as particularly and completely as you can and get him to sign and date the list. Otherwise he may later claim that you caused the damage.

G. SELF PROTECTION WHEN MOVING IN

When you are about to move in, take a look around. If there is anything at all wrong with the place—if there is any dirt or damage of any kind—get a few of the most responsible of your friends to take a look at it. This is so that, if necessary, they can later testify to the condition of the place when you moved in. Get them to write a simple little dated note (reminder) of what they saw. If at all possible, have a friend take a photograph of all defects. When developed, properly identify each photo on the back by location, date and signature. All notes and pictures should go into your file with your other records.

If you plan to attach cupboards, shelves, bookcases, air conditioners, room dividers or anything at all to the premises, you

January 1, 1977

Landlord *Smith Realty* and Tenant *Patricia Parker* make the following agreement:

1. Patricia Parker agrees to buy paint and painting supplies not to exceed a cost of $30 and to paint apartment #4 at 1500 Acorn Street, Cloverdale, California, on or before February 1, 1977 and to forward all receipts for painting supplies and paint to Smith Realty;

2. Smith Realty agrees to reduce payment due February 1, 1977 by $50 in consideration for the painting to be done by Patricia Parker and in addition to allow Patricia Parker to deduct the actual cost of paint and painting supplies not to exceed $30 from the rent payment due February 1, 1977.

3. The premises are being rented with the following defects:
    a. dent in oven door,
    b. gouge over fireplace in wall.

Smith Realty Company
By: B. C. Smith

Patricia Parker

should get something in writing from the landlord permitting you to install such things, and (if you plan it) to later remove them. By California law, anything which is nailed, screwed or bolted to the premises becomes the property of the landlord. If you remove the object when you leave, your landlord will have the right to recover compensation for any damages suffered to the premises and may also be able to recover the value of the object removed unless there is a written agreement to the contrary. In addition, most landlords are sensitive about having the premises altered without their consent and may get quite irritated if they discover changes after they have already been made.

1. LANDLORD-TENANT CHECKLIST

Another good self-protection device for both landlord and tenant involves taking an inventory of the condition of the premises at the time you move in, and then again when you move out. This means no more than making a brief written record of the condition of each room and having it signed by you and your landlord. Not only does the inventory give both of you an accurate record of the condition of the unit, but the act of making it provides a framework for communication and the resolution of potential disputes.

When filling out your checklist you will want to be as specific as possible. Thus you might state next to stove and refrigerator: "generally good, but oven greasy and refrigerator dirty". Be sure to note things like worn rugs, chipped enamel, holes in screens, dirty cabinets, etc. If you need more space than provided on your checklist form, make a separate writing for those items signed by both landlord and tenant and have it stapled to the checklist. You will find a tear-out checklist at the back of this book.

H. YOUR RESPONSIBILITIES AS A TENANT

1. COMPLY WITH YOUR LEASE OR RENTAL AGREEMENT

Your most important responsibility as a tenant is to comply with the provisions of your lease or rental agreement. If you do not, you may have to pay money to the landlord or you may be evicted, and sometimes both. Read your lease or agreement carefully to see what it requires you to do and prevents you from doing.

2. PAY YOUR RENT ON TIME

You must pay your rent on the day it is due. Most leases and rental agreements say rent is due on the first of the month. However, if the first falls on a Sunday or a legal holiday, then the law says that the rent can be paid on the next business day.*

If you do not pay your rent on time, you may have to pay a late charge, if your lease or rental agreement provides for this. Also, your landlord may serve upon you a "three-day notice" to pay your rent in three days or get out. If you do not comply with the three-day notice, he can then sue to evict you.

You are entitled to a written receipt whenever you pay your rent.** Be sure to get one, as this is proof that you paid your rent. Keep your receipts in a safe place.

3. KEEP THE PLACE CLEAN

The housing codes and almost all agreements require that you keep your place clean, safe and sanitary. You must properly dispose of all garbage and trash in your premises, placing it in the containers provided by the landlord.

4. REPAIR ANYTHING YOU BREAK

Anything damaged by you, other occupants or guests must be repaired at your expense, **unless** the damage resulted from "normal wear and tear" during ordinary use. If you sit on a chair and it breaks from old age, you do not have to repair or replace it. If, however, your child breaks the chair in a temper tantrum, you must pay for it.

I. ROOMMATES

Often two or more people rent a place together. The person (or

---

*Code of Civil Procedure Section 13; Government Code Section 6700 **et seq.**
**Civil Code Section 1499: "A debtor has a right to require from his creditor a written receipt for any property delivered in performance of his obligation."

people) signing the lease or rental agreement, or participating in the oral agreement if there is no writing, is responsible to the landlord for the **full** rent for the **full** term of the agreement unless there is a specific agreement to the contrary. This means that if two people sign a lease for a year and one of them leaves after six months, both are independently responsible for the full amount of the remaining rent, unless the place is, or can be, rerented (see chapter 7). The landlord will not care who he collects from and will try to get his money the easiest way possible, which normally will be from the remaining tenant.

If two or more people rent a place, but only one signs the agreement, only that person is liable for rent as far as the landlord is concerned.

EXAMPLE: John and Sue rent a unit on a month to month written rental agreement, both signing the agreement. After a few months, Sue leaves without giving 30 days notice. John then gives a proper 30 day notice and leaves a month later. Both John and Sue are responsible for all the last month's rent. The landlord will probably try and collect from John in Sue's absence. If John pays the full amount he would have the right to collect half the total amount from Sue if he can catch up with her.

J. CO-SIGNING LEASES

Some landlords have begun requiring a co-signor on leases and rental agreements as a condition of renting. Normally, they ask the co-signor to sign a contract saying that he will pay for any rent or damage losses that the tenants fail to pay. Several landlords have told us that inclusion of this sort of provision is mostly psychological and that they don't often sue the co-signor even if the original tenant defaults. Psychological or not, it is possible that a cosignor will be sued if the tenant defaults, so don't co-sign if you are not fully ready to pay.

IMPORTANT: Many co-signor clauses don't appear to be enforceable in court because they are so vague that they don't qualify as contracts. If a landlord and tenant change the terms of their rental agreement without the approval of the co-signor, he is no longer responsible.* Of course defenses that a tenant may raise (e.g., breach of the warranty of habitability) may be raised by the co-signor.

---

*See also Civil Code Section 2819; **Wexler** v. **McLucas**, 48 CA3 Supp. 9 (1975).

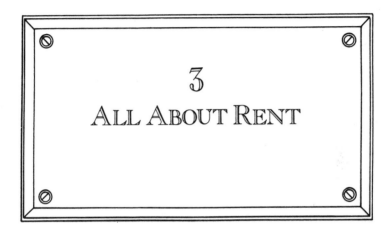

3
ALL ABOUT RENT

A. HOW MUCH CAN
THE LANDLORD CHARGE?

Legally the landlord can charge you as much rent as he can get, and he usually will. This may **not** be true if there is a "rent freeze" in effect when you read this (see Part D, below).

If you live in **public** housing, the rent can be no more than 25% of your income, **after** certain deductions are taken. The same is true if you live in private housing under the "leased housing" (or "Section 8") program run by your local housing authority. This is one reason why many people try hard to get into public housing or leased housing. If you don't know whether there are such programs in your community, call City Hall or the County Administration Building.

Needless to say, try to bargain a private landlord down on the rent he is asking, if you think you can.

B. WHEN IS RENT DUE?

Almost all leases and rental agreements provide that the rent for a period is due before the period starts. Thus, rent for use of the place in March would be due on March 1.

As we will see later, if you don't pay your rent on the day it is due, the landlord can then serve you with a "three-day notice," telling you to pay your rent in three days or get out. At the end of the three days, if you haven't paid your rent or left, he can sue you and get an eviction order, court costs, maybe his attorney's fees and up to three times the rent due (if he can prove that your refusal to vacate the premises was deliberate and intended).

If you run into trouble paying your rent on time, three days isn't much time to come up with it. You might expect such trouble if your income is from alimony and child support, welfare, or a job which might involve lay-offs or strikes. If this might happen to you, ask the landlord to put in the lease or rental agreement a provision that he will not serve a "three-day notice" on you until some time (like ten days or twenty days) after the first of the month. If he objects, write the provision so that it gives you the extra time only if your income is temporarily cut off or delayed, and maybe he will accept that.

C. CALIFORNIA RENT LAW

Under California law, rent cannot be raised during a **lease** unless the written terms of the lease itself specifically allow the increase. Rent can be increased under a written or oral rental agreement if proper written notice is given to the tenant (the various rental agreements are described fully in Chapter 2, Part B). Where rent is paid monthly, written notice must be given at least 30 days prior to the increase.[*] Oral notice of rent increases is not legally sufficient. California law allows a landlord renting under an oral or written agreement to raise the rent as much as he wishes in most

---

*Civil Code section 827

circumstances The exception to this rule is that rent cannot be raised as a retaliation because the tenant has notified public authorities of substantial code violations, nor can it be raised within 60 days after he withholds rent in order to fix a major defect (see chapter 6).

D. RENT CONTROL

Some states have at times enacted "rent control laws," which limit the rent landlords can charge. The federal government had a "rent freeze" in effect in 1972, but the freeze was later lifted.

California presently has no rent control laws effective throughout the state, but it is legally possible for cities to decide to enact rent control on a local basis. In 1972, a group of Berkeley citizens, led by the Berkeley Tenants' Organizing Committee (see p. 144), was concerned about rising rents driving low-income people out of the city. They requested the city council to enact a rent control law, but the council refused. The group then started an "initiative" drive to get enough signatures on a petition to have the issue put before the voters. They got the signatures, the issue was voted on at an election, and the rent control law was passed. It provided for the election of a five-member "Rent Control Board" which would allow rent increases to landlords only upon a showing that the increase would be justified (e.g., by cost increases). Soon after this law was enacted, some Berkeley landlords challenged it in court.

In **Birkenfeld v. City of Berkeley,** 17 Cal. 3d 129 (1976), the California Supreme Court held that cities (and counties) can enact rent control on a local basis, and they can do so through the initiative process. The Court held, however, that the Berkeley law was invalid because it did not provide a mechanism by which landlords could get authority to raise rents in a reasonable time.

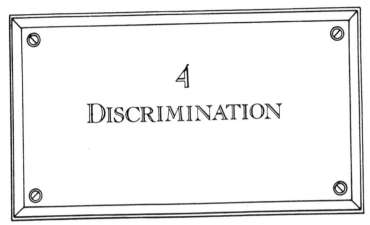

4
DISCRIMINATION

It is illegal throughout the state for a landlord to refuse to rent to you or impose harsher terms on you because of your race, natural origin or ancestry, religion, sex, marital status, or because you are physically disabled.* It is also illegal for a landlord to discriminate against a member of one race because they associate with members of a different race.**

A move is underway to ban discrimination against families with children. Berkeley and San Francisco have already done so.*** And the California Attorney General has issued an opinion (No. 5075-6, August 21, 1975) stating that no landlord in California may discriminate against children without good reason (such as the fact that a building was designed and built to serve elderly people).

A. HOW TO TELL IF
A LANDLORD IS DISCRIMINATING

Occasionally an apartment house manager—and rarely a landlord himself—will tell you that he will not rent to blacks, Spanish-surnamed people, Asians, etc. This does not happen often any

---

*Racial, religious, ethnic, sex and marital status discrimination are forbidden by California Health and Safety Code Sections 35720 **et seq.** California Civil Code Sections 51 and 52 (Unruh Civil Rights Act); **Jones** v. **Alfred H. Mayer Co.,** 392 U. S. 409 (1968); 42 U. S. Code Sections 3601 **et seq.** (Fair Housing Act of 1968). Sex discrimination is forbidden by California Civil Code Section 51 and 52. Physical disability discrimination is forbidden by California Civil Code Section 54.1. Marital status discrimination includes discrimination against unmarried couples, **Atkisson** v. **Kern County Housing Authority,** 59 Cal. App. 3d. 89 (1976).

Winchell v. **English, 133 Cal. Rptr. 20 (Ct. App. 1976).

***San Francisco - ordinance number 320-75. Berkeley - ordinance number 4835. Violations should be reported to the District Attorney in San Francisco and Alameda County respectively.

more, because these people are learning that they can be penalized if it is proved that they are discriminating.

Today, most landlords who wish to discriminate try to be subtle about it. When you phone to see if a place is still available, the landlord may say it has been filled if he hears a southern or Mexican accent. It he says it is vacant, then when you come to look at it and he sees that you are black, Chicano, etc., he may say it has just been rented. Or, he may say he requires a security deposit equal to three month's rent, which he "forgot to put in the ad." Or, he may say that the ad misprinted the rent, which is $175 not $125. Many variations on these themes can be played.

IF you suspect that the landlord is discriminating against you, it is important that you do some things to check it out. For example, if you think he is asking for a high rent or security deposit just to get rid of you, ask other tenants what they pay. The best way to check is to run a "test." Have someone who would not have trouble with discrimination (for example, a white Protestant) revisit the place soon after you do and ask if it is available and, if so, on what terms. If the response is better, the landlord was probably discriminating against you. Be sure that your friend's references, type of job and life style are similar to yours, so that the landlord cannot later say he took your friend and turned you down because of this difference.

B. WHAT TO DO ABOUT DISCRIMINATION

There are several different legal approaches to the problems raised by discrimination. If you are a victim of such discrimination, the next few paragraphs should be read carefully in order to decide which approach best fits your situation. Regardless of what you do, if you really want to live in the place, you must act fast, otherwise he will rent it to someone else before he can be stopped.

1. THE FAIR EMPLOYMENT PRACTICE COMMISSION (FEPC):

The State of California Fair Employment Practice Commission (FEPC) takes complaints on discrimination in rental housing. This Commission enforces laws which prohibit housing discrimination, in addition to their other work, and has the power to order up to $1,000 damages for a tenant who has been discriminated against.

San Francisco
P. O. Box 603
Golden Gate Avenue
Phone: 557-2005

Los Angeles
322 West First Street
Phone: 620-2610

Fresno
2550 Mariposa Street
Phone: 488-5373

San Diego
1350 Front Street
Phone: 232-4361, Ext. 285

Sacramento
926 J Street
Phone: 445-9918

If you believe that you have been discriminated against, you can contact the office nearest you. You will be asked to fill out a complaint form and an investigator will be assigned to your case. You must file your complaint within 60 days of the date of the violation or the date when you first learn of the violation. The FEPC investigator will try to work the problem out through compromise and conciliation. If this fails the Commission may conduct hearings and maybe take the matter to court. It has been our experience that in recent years the FEPC has been slack in enforcing anti-discrimination housing laws. Therefore, before going to the FEPC, we would recommend that you consult a private attorney.

2. THE UNITED STATES DEPARTMENT OF HOUSING AND URBAN DEVELOPMENT (Racial or Religious Discrimination only)

You can also lodge a complaint with the U. S. Department of Housing and Urban Development (HUD). This federal agency has most of the same powers as does the state FEPC but must let the FEPC act on a case first. The HUD equal opportunity office for California is located at 450 Golden Gate Avenue in San Francisco (phone: 566-3840). HUD's powers of investigation and sanctions are similar to those of FEPC. The experience of the authors has been that HUD is far more militant in going after discriminating landlords than is FEPC. However, the fact that HUD can't act until 30 days after FEPC has received the complaint reduces their efficiency a great deal.

3. SUE THE DISCRIMINATING LANDLORD

We think that the most effective thing you can do is to see a lawyer and sue the landlord. If you have been discriminated against because of sex, race, religion, physical disability or marital status, a law suit may be brought in State Court. Suits in Federal Court only work for racial or religious discrimination. If you can prove your case, you will almost certainly be given the right to occupy the dwelling in question and will also be eligible to recover money damages. Many, if not most attorneys, will have had little experience with discrimination law suits. This is particularly true of law suits brought in Federal Court. Rather than try to find an attorney at random, you would be wise to check with an organization in your area dedicated to civil rights and fighting discrimination. They will undoubtedly be able to direct you to a sympathetic attorney.

Attorneys have become more interested in taking these cases in the last few years, because the amount of money that can be recovered is now substantial. For racial or religious discrimination, you can sue in federal court and collect damages to compensate you for your loss as well as substantial punitive damages and attorney's fees.* For discrimination based on sex, disability or marital status, you can sue in state court and collect damages to compensate you for your loss and a penalty of $250.** If you ask the FEPC to take your case and they decline and you then sue the landlord and win, you may also recover attorney's fees in state court.***

If you have any trouble preparing your case, need advice about whether you have been discriminated against, or just want to talk to someone about housing discrimination, volunteers will help you at your local Fair Housing Organization. For the office nearest you contact:

Fair Housing Conference of So. Calif.
4034 Buckingham Road
Los Angeles, California 90008

Mid Peninsula Citizens for Fair Housing
457 Kingsley Avenue
Palo Alto, California 94301

---

*42 USC Section 3612; **Morales** v. **Haines,** 486 F. 2d 880 (7th Cir., 1973); **Lee** v. **Southern Home Sites Corp.,** 429 F. 2d 290 (5th Cir., 1970).

**Civil Code sections 51 and 52.

***Health and Safety Code section 35731.

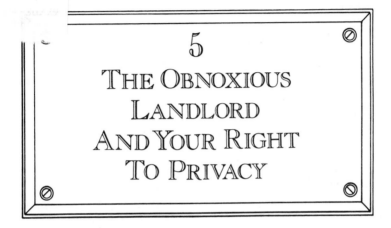

5
THE OBNOXIOUS LANDLORD AND YOUR RIGHT TO PRIVACY

A. YOUR RIGHTS

Some landlords can get pretty obnoxious. This is also true of plumbers, butchers and English teachers, but since this book is for tenants we will concentrate on just the landlords. Typically, problems arise with those kinds of landlords who cannot stop fidgeting and fussing over their property. Normally, smaller landlords develop this problem to a greater extent than do the bigger, more commercial ones. Nosey landlords are always hanging around or coming by, trying to invite themselves in to look around and generally being pesty. Sometimes you may run into a manager on a power trip.

If your landlord is difficult or unpleasant to deal with, he can make your life miserable and you may not be able to do anything about it. There is no law which protects you from a disagreeable personality, and, if you have no lease, you are especially unprotected from all but the most outrageous invasions of privacy or trespass. Things can get really unpleasant, but if your right to privacy and peaceful occupancy are not disturbed, you may have to grin and bear it or look for another place.*

The landlord may enter your dwelling without your consent only in the following cases:

(a) In an emergency;
(b) To make necessary or agreed repairs, decorations, alterations, or improvements, supply necessary services, or show the place to prospective or actual purchasers, mortgagers, tenants, workmen or contractors;
(c) Where the tenant has moved out;
(d) Pursuant to a court order.

Unless there is an emergency, the landlord cannot enter outside of "normal business hours" unless the tenant consents at the time of entry.

The law provides that the landlord shall not abuse his right of entry or use it to harass the tenant. The landlord must give the tenant reasonable notice of his intent to enter (24 hours is presumed to be reasonable), except in an emergency or where it is otherwise impracticable to give such notice.

Civil Code Section 1953 provides that any lease or rental agreement provision trying to waive or modify the tenant's rights under section 1954 is void.

EXAMPLE: Landlord calls tenant at nine o'clock in the morning and says he wants to show the apartment at eleven o'clock the same morning. This is inconvenient to the tenant. Can the tenant refuse to let the landlord in? Yes.

---

*Recently a court allowed a suit by a tenant alleging that a landlord was guilty of the intentional infliction of emotional distress. The court found that it was necessary to prove four things in this sort of suit: 1) outrageous conduct on the part of the landlord; 2) intention to cause or reckless disregard of the probability of causing emotional distress; 3) severe emotional suffering; and 4) actual suffering or emotional distress. **Newby** v. **Alto Riviera Apartments,** 131 Cal. Rptr. 547. 1976.

B. WHAT TO DO ABOUT IT

As you have probably figured out by now, it is one thing to have a right, and quite another thing to get the benefits of it. This is especially true for tenants. If you set about aggressively demanding your rights, you may end up with a notice to vacate. Your position is slightly better if you have a lease, but even then the landlord will possibly take the first opportunity to find a breach in the fine print provisions and try to get rid of you. It is also generally true in life that you can rarely accomplish good results with hard words; never forget that the landlord holds most of the cards. This doesn't mean not to be firm or determined, but rather, not to be offensive.

If you experience any kind of problem at all during your tenancy—be it housing conditions, sanitation, disrepair, nosey landlord, etc.—it is only common sense to begin with a polite call to your landlord about the problem. After all, he may merely be ignorant of your point of view, and may be willing to respond to a request, especially if nicely put. If, after a reasonable time, there has been no satisfactory response, put it in writing. Mention your previous oral request by the date, and ask again for prompt correction. Keep a copy for your records. If you have a manager through whom you must work, send duplicate copies to the manager and landlord.

Diplomacy varies according to the circumstances and personalities involved. In negotiating with your landlord, it is important to always behave in a way which is most likely to convince him that in you he has as good and reliable a tenant as he can ever hope to find. This is the main strength of your position. Things will be much easier if he likes you and thinks that you can understand his problems and characteristics. It is very important for later possible action that you communicate in writing, keep copies and at all times conduct yourself reasonably.

When your best efforts have continued to the point that you consider them to have failed (how long this is depends upon how urgent or objectionable the problem is) you are faced with but a few choices: (a) you can do nothing and just live with the problem; or, (b) move away; or, (c) bluff (pretend you are going to get serious); or (d) stay and really fight it out.

If you choose (c) or (d), send the landlord a letter telling him "finally" that if there is not an immediate positive response you will seek legal advice, go to appropriate public authorities, or do whatever else is required to secure your rights. In making your decision of which alternative to follow, never forget that if you make the landlord angry enough, he'll make the decision for you, and you'll have to face the additional problems of a notice to vacate. At this point, it might be a good idea to see a lawyer, at least for advice and information (see Chapter 1, Part C).

One difficulty with a law suit against a landlord guilty of trespass is that it is hard to prove much in the way of money damages. Assuming you can prove that the trespass occurred, the judge will probably readily agree that you have been wronged, but he may award you very little money. Most likely he will figure that you have not been harmed much by the fact that your landlord walked on your rug and opened and closed your door. However, if you can show a repeated pattern of trespass, or even one clear example of outrageous conduct, you may be able to get a substantial recovery. Unless you have a fairly good case, a law suit may cost you more than your claim is worth. However, on a limited basis you may find it financially worthwhile to hire a lawyer to contact your landlord to tell him to stop his improper conduct. You also may want to consider bringing a suit yourself in small claims court.

If your landlord comes onto your property or into your home and harms you in any way, or threatens you or damages any of your property, see an attorney. You should also report the matter to the police. Some California police departments have taken the excellent step of setting up special landlord/tenant units. The officers and legal experts in these units have been given special training in landlord/tenant law and are often helpful in compromising disputes and setting a landlord straight who has taken illegal measures against a tenant. Oakland is one such city. Try to get your local police department to follow suit.

Probably the time that a landlord is most likely to trespass is when the tenant has failed to pay his rent. The landlord, faced with the necessity of paying a lot of money to legally get a tenant to move out, may resort to threats or even force. While it may be understandable that a landlord in this situation should be mad at the tenant, this is no justification for illegal acts (we discuss illegal conduct during evictions in Chapter 9, Part A).

All threats, intimidation and any physical attacks on the tenant should be reported to the police. Of course it is illegal for the landlord to come on the property and do such things as take off windows and doors, turn off the utilities or change the locks. If this is done the tenant should see an attorney at once. Do not over-react when a landlord gets hostile. While a tenant has the right to take reasonable steps to protect himself, his family and his possessions from harm, the steps must be reasonably related to the threat. The wisest thing to do whenever you fear you or your property may be harmed is to call the police.

```
┌─────────────────────────────────────────┐
│  ◎                                    ◎  │
│                   6                      │
│           SUBSTANDARD                    │
│        HOUSING CONDITIONS                │
│           HOW TO GET                     │
│          REPAIRS MADE                    │
│  ◎                                    ◎  │
└─────────────────────────────────────────┘
```

From time to time things are likely to go wrong with any property. Most landlords are willing to repair and maintain their places because they don't want them to get too rundown, but sometimes you find landlords being slow and reluctant to fulfill their responsibilities. If you are having problems with your landlord in this regard, read Part A and make sure you know what your rights are, then consider all the alternatives in Part B before you decide how to start.

A. YOUR RIGHTS—THE LANDLORD'S DUTY

Under the State Housing Law and local housing codes, the landlord is required to maintain the building in a sound structural condition. This includes maintaining the roof, plumbing, and heating facilities. In addition, he is required to maintain those parts of the building and grounds which he controls (such as the stairways and halls) in a clean, sanitary and safe condition, including getting rid of insects, rodents and other pests.

The landlord's duties under the State Housing Law are spelled out in great detail in Chatper 2, part D, in the section on inspecting the premises. The requirements mentioned in that section apply not only when the landlord is trying to rent the place, but also during the time you live there.

The State Housing Law says that the landlord has these duties even if he tries to impose them on you in the lease or rental agreement.

It is possible that the local government in the area in which you live will have laws which are even more strict than those enacted by the State. If you have a problem, don't hesitate to call the local Building or Health Inspector to check on this.

The landlord is also required, of course, to make any repairs he agreed to make in your lease or rental agreement.

B. GETTING REPAIRS MADE

Whenever you have a significant problem with rental property, whether it is major or minor, you should report it to your landlord. While this may seem obvious, it apparently is not. Hopefully, once your landlord (or his authorized agent, such as the apartment manager or real estate company) has been told of your problem it will be corrected promptly. What constitutes "promptness" varies a lot with the circumstances involved. It may be reasonable for a landlord to take a week to fix a furnace in Tucson, Arizona in the summer, while it would be unreasonable for him to take two days to fix a furnace in Green Bay, Wisconsin in the winter. In deciding what is reasonable, try to be fair and to take into consideration any special problems that the landlord is having such as the inability to get a part. Try to propose sensible suggestions to your landlord if it looks as if an unavoidable delay is inevitable. For example, if the furnace breaks and it is going to take a couple of days to get it fixed, you might ask the landlord to make an empty unit available to you in the interim or to pay for a motel room for you for a few days.

If you get no response or what you believe is an inadequate response to your request that repairs be made, you should then send or give the landlord a written notice of the defects, keeping a carbon or xerox copy for your records. Even though calling on the telephone is easier, you should give this notice in writing so that you have a record for later use if necessary. Your note might go something like this:

1500 Acorn Street, #4
Cloverdale, California
March 14, 1977

Smith Realty Co.
10 Jones Street
Cloverdale, California

Dear Sirs:

I reside in apartment #4 at 1500 Acorn Street and regularly pay my rent to your office.

On March 11, 1977 the water heater in my unit failed to function. On that date I notified your manager Mr. Robert Jackson of the problem. He called P. G. & E. on that date and they sent a man out who put a tag on the machine saying that it was no longer serviceable or safe and that it should be replaced. I gave Mr. Jackson a copy of the P. G. & E. slip on March 12, 1977 and he said that he would see about having the heater replaced immediately.

So far the heater has not been replaced and no one has told me when it will be. I am sure you know that it is a real hardship to be without hot water. I will appreciate hearing from you as soon as possible. My telephone at work is 657-4111.

Very truly yours,

Patricia Parker

Occasionally a polite but firm approach does not work. In that case, you are simply faced with the fact that the landlord is not going to make needed repairs voluntarily. There are some legal steps that a tenant can take to get major defects repaired, but before deciding anything you should sit down with yourself and figure out what you are getting into.

If you need to get repairs made you have several approaches available to you:

1. Withhold your rent payments.

2. Get help from the local authorities.

3. Pay for repairs out of your rent.

4. Sue the landlord.

5. Stay and forget the whole thing.

6. Move out.

Read the discussion below on each one of them before deciding what to do. Keep it in mind that any method you use to pressure and force your landlord into making repairs can possibly escalate into a long and troublesome conflict. The landlord is almost certain to get alienated on a personal level, and he may start looking for the first excuse to get rid of you for being a troublesome tenant. There are protections against retaliation, which we discuss below, but they have definite limits. Ultimately, what you decide to do depends upon all the facts and personalities in your own particular case. After reading the sections below, if you are still uncertain or unclear, then you should consider getting advice from an attorney (see Chapter 1, Part C).

1. RENT WITHHOLDING

Under a recent decision of the California Supreme Court,* California tenants now have a powerful new weapon to use in their battles to get substandard housing improved. Previously, tenants have been relatively weak in this area, but now the tables are turning.

Under the rules of this new court decision, whenever the landlord fails to comply with housing codes by refusing to make proper repairs, the tenant now has the right to withhold rent payments (and, eventually, he may even get to keep part of it) **if** the circumstances are right and if he properly asserts his rights.**

All leases and rental agreements are now deemed by the law to include an "implied warranty of habitability." This means that whether it is actually written down or not, and whether he likes it or not, the landlord is required as a condition of any rental agreement to maintain the place in a habitable condition, as defined by the Housing Code.

If your landlord violates ("breaches") his obligation to you under this warranty, you may have the right to withhold rent payments **if** his breach was "material." What is a ."material" breach has yet to be clearly defined by the law, but here are some guidelines the court has set out. Both the seriousness of the defect and the length of time it persists are relevant factors in deciding if it was material. Minor code violations will not be considered material. Nor will violations which do not affect the tenant's apartment or the common areas he uses. Thus, failure to correct heavy rat infestation for a month would be clearly material, while a few ants which came in on one occasion when it rained would not. No heat for a week in January might be material, while a doorway an inch lower than allowed by the codes would not. Until the rules on this issue are more fully developed, you will just have to use common sense as to what is "material."***

---

*Green v. Superior Court, 10 Cal. 3d 616 (Jan. 15, 1974).
If the defects were present **when the tenant moved in, it is not yet clear what legal remedies the tenant has. The Court in **Green** did not decide this issue.
***Courts have generally found that the conditions set out as untenantable in section 1941.1 also apply here. See page 82.

If the breach is material, you may exercise your right to withhold rent only if (a) the defect was not caused by you, anyone living with you or a guest or visitor of yours; (b) you gave the landlord notice of the defects and allowed him a reasonable time to repair them. If you can, use the form "Notice to Repair" set out on page 86, below. You are not legally required to give a written notice—an oral demand will do, but it won't be as easy to prove later on.

If a "reasonable time" passes and the landlord has failed to properly make the repairs, do not make your next rent payment. Although not required by law, it may be a good idea to give the landlord a second note at this time telling him what you are doing. It might look like the notice on the following page.

If the landlord then makes the repairs, you must resume your regular rent payments the next month, but you do **not** have to pay him the full amount of the rent you already withheld. You only owe him a "reasonable rent" out of that. What is a "reasonable rent" depends on the circumstances and has **not** yet been clearly defined by the law. In one New Jersey case where the landlord had failed to provide heat, hot water, elevator service and incinerator use, the court required the tenant to pay only 75% of the agreed rent.* If you and your landlord can't agree on this, you could keep the money and let him take you to court if he wants to. On the other hand, it may not be worth the trouble. If you do keep the extra money, and if he does go to court, and if you prove that he materially breached his "implied warranty of habitability" and you gave him notice to repair and he failed to do so in a reasonable time, the court will decide what is a reasonable rent and make you pay only that amount.

If you follow the procedures in this section, then when you refuse to pay your rent on time, it is quite likely that the landlord will give you a "three-day notice" to pay your rent in three days or get out. Then, when you fail to do either, he'll sue to have you evicted (see Chapter 9 for a full discussion of the eviction proce-

---

*Academy Spires, Inc. v. Brown, 111 N.J. Spr. 477, 268 A.2d 556, 562 (1970).

NOTICE OF RENT WITHHOLDING

To _____, Landlord of the premises
located at _____ .

NOTICE IS HEREBY GIVEN that because of your failure to comply with your implied warranty of habitability by refusing to repair certain defects on the premises, as previously demanded of you, within a reasonable time after such demand, the undersigned tenant has elected to withhold this month's rent in accordance with California law. Rent payments will be resumed in the future, as they become due, only after said defects have been properly repaired.

Dated: _____

_____
(Signature of tenant)

Authority: *Green* v. *Superior Court,* 10 Cal. 3d 616
(Jan. 15, 1974).

dure). While normally he would easily win such a suit, in this case you have a good defense, and he will not be allowed to evict you if you can prove that he materially breached his implied warranty of habitability.

When you raise this defense in your case, the judge may then order you to make future rent payments into court until the law suit is concluded. (He may **not** order you to pay into court the rent you already withheld.)

At the end of the trial, if you have proved your case, the court will decide what was a "reasonable rent" while the defects on the premises were not corrected. When this is decided, that portion of the rent money which you paid into court which represents "reasonable rent" will be paid to the landlord, and the balance will be returned to you. Also, the landlord will receive a judgment for the reasonable rent portion of the rent you withheld. He will **not** get an eviction order, and he should not recover his attorney's fees or court costs either, since you really won the case (in fact, **you** should be able to get **your** attorney's fees and court costs).

If you do not have a lease, the landlord might try to get you out simply by giving you a 30-day notice to vacate (rather than a three-day notice to pay the rent or get out). If you refuse to move and can prove in the eviction law suit he brings that he gave you the notice to retaliate against you for rightfully withholding your rent, then this might well be held to an attempted illegal "retaliation eviction" and you will not be evicted. Actually, the California courts have not yet dealt with retaliation in this type of situation, but a recent case from the District of Columbia held this kind of retaliation to be illegal. **Robinson** v. **Diamond Housing Corp.,** 463 F. 24 853 (D.C. Cir. 1972).

Rent withholding is a powerful strategy. If all goes according to the law stated above you can stay in the premises, withhold rent and win eviction actions until the premises are brought up to code. Unfortunately, you might get into a law suit and require an attorney's services. Quite often, however, the written threat of rent withholding is sufficient to solve the problem.

2. GO TO THE LOCAL AUTHORITIES

The State Housing Law and local housing codes are supposed to be enforced by a city or county agency. Codes are usually enforced by an agency called the Building Inspection Department (or some similar name). Violations creating immediate health hazards (such as rats or broken toilets) are also enforced by the Health Department. Violations creating fire hazards (such as trash in the basement) are also enforced by the Fire Department.

These agencies have the power to close the building and even demolish it if the landlord will not comply with their orders to correct code violations. They very seldom go to this extreme, however. Usually they inspect the building, send a letter to the landlord ordering him to make repairs, and later reinspect the building and send more letters until the landlord complies.

This sort of pressure works on many landlords, so your reporting code violations to the agency and asking for an inspection can sometimes help you. If you decide to do this, it is best to go to the agency and make your complaint in writing.

There are, however, some things to watch out for before deciding to report code violations.

First, if the place is **really** bad, constituting a real health or fire hazard which the landlord will be unable to remedy soon, the agency just might close the building down, kicking you out in the process. This doesn't help you, unless you just want to get back at the landlord. If you are afraid this might happen, see if you can find out the name of someone in the agency who is friendly to tenants. Call this person and see what the agency is likely to do.

Second, if the landlord owns a lot of slum property or has been in this business for a while, he probably knows what to do to keep the agency off his back. He may be friendly with the building inspectors. He may know how to take appeals which can delay enforcement of the codes for years. He may make a few repairs and let the others go, knowing just how much it takes to temporarily satisfy the agency that he is "trying." The landlord is less likely to get away with these tricks if there is a real health or fire hazard, like rats or open gasoline on the premises. The Health or Fire Departments will usually be tougher than the Building Inspec-

---

* Another remedy was set up in 1974. If the landlord has failed for six months or more to comply with agency orders to repair, the enforcement agency is required to notify the state's Franchise Tax Board. The Board then denies the landlord any deduction on his state income tax form for interest, taxes, or depreciation on the building. California Revenue & Taxation Code sections 17299 and 24436.5. So far, not many agencies are reporting violations to the Board, so you may need to push them a bit.

tion Department.

Third, there is a danger that the landlord will find out that you reported him to the agency and will try to evict you because of this. This is called a "retaliatory eviction." The landlord will usually do this simply by giving you a 30-day notice terminating your month-to-month tenancy, giving no reason for his doing so. Or, he might give you a 30-day notice that your rent is being increased as an indirect way of getting you out.

Retaliatory evictions for reporting code violations are illegal,* so if you refuse to get out and the landlord sues to evict you and you prove he is doing it because you reported the code violations, you will win the law suit. The problem is that **you** have the burden of proof. If the landlord can show that he is evicting you for some good reason (for example, you violated the lease), you might lose. However, by attempting a retaliatory eviction, the landlord is taking a chance too. If you get out because of his 30-day notice but can prove it was retaliatory, you can sue him for money damages later.**

If you have a lease, you are pretty well protected from retaliatory evictions, since the landlord must prove a good reason to kick you out before your lease is up. If you have only a month-to-month rental agreement, you do face the danger of retaliatory evictions, **unless** you have a provision like Paragraph 16 of the Model Month-to-Month Rental Agreement in Chapter 2 of this Handbook. That paragraph requires the landlord to state his reasons when trying to terminate your tenancy or increase the rent, and to prove these reasons are true if you question them.

When deciding whether to withhold rent, sue the landlord, or take other action against him, you may wish to find out if he has had trouble with the housing code inspection before. In the past, many code inspectors have refused to show tenants their records without the landlord's permission. A new statute, however, ex-

---

*Schweiger v. Superior Court, 3 Cal. 3d 507, 90 Cal. Rptr. 729 (1970). See also Moskovitz, Retaliatory Eviction—A New Doctrine in California, 46 Calif. State Bar Journal 23 (1971); Civil Code Section 1942.5.
**Aweeka v. Bonds, 20 Cal. App. 3d 278 (1971).

pressly declares that all records of notices and orders directed to the landlord concerning serious code violations (those listed in Civil Code §1941.1, see page 82) and the inspector's acts regarding those violations are **public records.** Government Code §6254.7(c). Every citizen has the right to inspect any public record. Government Code §6253.

3. REPAIR IT YOURSELF

Where your landlord refuses to make repairs, California law gives you the right to make the repairs yourself (or hire someone to do them) and deduct the cost from your next month's rent. There are, however, some restrictions on this right, and there are certain procedures you must follow to exercise this right. The law on this subject is stated in California Civil Code Sections 1941-1942.5. For your convenience, these sections are set out in their entirety on the following pages.

a.   Restrictions on the Right to Repair and Deduct

First, this remedy can be used only for certain defects. It can be used only if your place substantially lacks any of the following (C.C. 1941.1):

- effective waterproofing and weather protection of roof and exterior walls, including unbroken windows and doors;
- plumbing facilities maintained in good working order;
- a water system which produces hot and cold running water;
- heating facilities maintained in good working order;
- lighting and wiring maintained in good working order;
- building and grounds clean of trash, rodents and vermin;
- an adequate number of garbage cans and trash barrels, kept in clean condition and good repair;

[text continued on page 85]

Civil Code

§ 1941. [Lessor to make dwelling-house fit for its purpose.]
The lessor of a building intended for the occupation of human beings must, in the absence of an agreement to the contrary, put it into a condition fit for such occupation, and repair all subsequent dilapidations thereof, which render it untenantable, except such as are mentioned in section nineteen hundred and twenty-nine.

§ 1941.1. [Same: When dwelling untenantable.]
A dwelling shall be deemed untenantable for purposes of Section 1941 if it substantially lacks any of the following affirmative standard characteristics:

(a) Effective waterproofing and weather protection of roof and exterior walls, including unbroken windows and doors.

(b) Plumbing facilities which conformed to applicable law in effect at the time of installation, maintained in good working order.

(c) A water supply approved under applicable law, which is under the control of the tenant, capable of producing hot and cold running water, or a system which is under the control of the landlord, which produces hot and cold running water, furnished to appropriate fixtures, and connected to a sewage disposal system approved under applicable law.

(d) Heating facilities which conformed with applicable law at the time of installation, maintained in good working order.

(e) Electrical lighting, with wiring and electrical equipment which conformed with applicable law at the time of installation, maintained in good working order.

(f) Building, grounds and appurtenances at the time of the commencement of the lease or rental agreement in every part clean, sanitary, and free from all accumulations of debris, filth, rubbish, garbage, rodents and vermin, and all areas under control of the landlord kept in every part clean, sanitary, and free from all accumulations of debris, filth, rubbish, garbage, rodents, and vermin.

(g) An adequate number of appropriate receptacles for garbage and rubbish, in clean condition and good repair at the time of the commencement of the lease or rental agreement, with the landlord providing appropriate serviceable receptacles thereafter, and being responsible for the clean condition and good repair of such receptacles under his control.

(h) Floors, stairways, and railings maintained in good repair.

§ 1941.2. [Same: Tenant's violations as excusing landlord's duties under §§ 1941 or 1942.]
(a) No duty on the part of the lessor shall arise under Section 1941 or 1942 if the lessee is in substantial violation of any of the following affirmative obligations:

(1) To keep that part of the premises which he occupies and uses clean and sanitary as the condition of the premises permits.

(2) To dispose from his dwelling unit of all rubbish, garbage and other waste, in a clean and sanitary manner.

(3) To properly use and operate all electrical, gas and plumbing fixtures and keep them as clean and sanitary as their condition permits.

(4) Not to permit any person on the premises, with his permission, to willfully or wantonly destroy, deface, damage, impair or remove any part of the structure or dwelling unit or the facilities, equipment, or appurtenances thereto, nor himself do any such thing.

(5) To occupy the premises as his abode, utilizing portions thereof for living, sleeping, cooking or dining purposes only which were respectively designed or intended to be used for such occupancies.

(b) Paragraphs (1) and (2) of subdivision (a) shall not apply if the lessor has expressly agreed in writing to perform the act or acts mentioned therein.

§ 1942. [When lessee may make repairs, etc.]

(a) If within a reasonable time after notice to the lessor, of dilapidations which he ought to repair, he neglects to do so, the lessee may repair the same himself, where the cost of such repairs *does* not require an expenditure greater than one month's rent of the premises, and deduct the expenses of such repairs from the rent, or the lessee may vacate the premises, in which case he shall be discharged from further payment of rent, or performance of other conditions. *This remedy shall not be available to the lessee more than once in any 12-month period.*

(b) For the purposes of this section, if a lessee acts to repair and deduct after the 30th day following notice, he is presumed to have acted after a reasonable time. The presumption established by this subdivision is a presumption affecting the burden of producing evidence.

§ 1942.1. [Same: Agreement to waive tenant's rights under §§ 1941 or 1942: Arbitration.]

Any agreement by a lessee of a dwelling waiving or modifying his rights under Section 1941 or 1942 shall be void as contrary to public policy with respect to any condition which renders the premises untenantable, except that the lessor and the lessee may agree that the lessee shall undertake to improve, repair or maintain all or stipulated portions of the dwelling as part of the consideration for rental.

The lessor and lessee may, if an agreement is in writing, set forth the provisions of Sections 1941 to 1942.1, inclusive, and provide that any controversy relating to a condition of the premises claimed to make them untenantable may by application of either party be submitted to arbitration, pursuant to the provisions of Title 9 (commencing with Section 1280), Part 3 of the Code of Civil Procedure, and that the costs of such arbitration shall be apportioned by the arbitrator between the parties.

§ 1942.5. [Same: Tenant's remedy for retaliation for exercising rights or filing complaint.]

(a) If the lessor has as his dominant purpose retaliation against the lessee because of the exercise by the lessee of his rights under this chapter or because of his complaint to an appropriate governmental agency as to tenantability of a dwelling, and if the lessee of a dwelling is not in default as to the payment of his rent, the lessor may not recover possession of a dwelling in any action or proceeding, cause the lessee to quit involuntarily, increase the rent, or decrease any services, within 60 days:

(1) After the date upon which the lessee, in good faith, has given notice pursuant to Section 1942; or

(2) After the date upon which the lessee, in good faith, has filed a written complaint, with an appropriate governmental agency, of which the lessor has notice, for the purpose of obtaining correction of a condition relating to tenantability; or

(3) After the date of an inspection or issuance of a citation, resulting from a written complaint described in paragraph (2) of which the lessor did not have notice; or

(4) After entry of judgment or the signing of an arbitration award, if any, when in the judicial proceeding or arbitration the issue of tenantability is determined adversely to the lessor.

In each instance, the 60-day period shall run from the latest applicable date referred to in paragraphs (1) to (4), inclusive.

(b) A lessee may not invoke the provisions of this section more than once in any 12-month period.

(c) Nothing in this section shall be construed as limiting in any way the exercise by the lessor of his rights under any lease or agreement or any law pertaining to the hiring of property or his right to do any of the acts described in subdivision (a) for any lawful cause. Any waiver by a lessee of his rights under this section shall be void as contrary to public policy.

(d) Notwithstanding the provisions of subdivisions (a) to (c), inclusive, a lessor may recover possession of a dwelling and do any of the other acts described in subdivision (a) within the period or periods prescribed therein if the notice of termination, rent increase, or other act, and any pleading or statement of issues in an arbitration, if any, states the ground upon which the lessor, in good faith, seeks to recover possession, increase rent, or do any of the other acts described in subdivision (a). If such statement be controverted, the lessor shall establish its truth at the trial or other hearing.

- floors, stairways and railings maintained in good repair.

Second, you are allowed to use this remedy only if **you** are not in substantial violation of any of the following duties (C.C. 1941.2):

- to keep your premises clean (unless the landlord has agreed to do this);
- to properly dispose of your garbage and trash (unless the landlord has agreed to do this);
- to properly use all electrical, gas and plumbing fixtures and keep them as clean as their condition permits;
- not to permit any person on the premises with your permission to willfully damage the presmises or the facilities, or to do so yourself;
- to use each room only for the purpose for which it was intended (for example, you can't sleep in the dining room).

Finally, you can use this remedy only is you have not used it against this landlord in the prior 12 months.

b. How to Exercise Your Right to Repair and Deduct

If you come within the above restrictions, you can use your repair and deduct remedy.

To do so, you must first notify the landlord of the defects he should repair. You should put this in writing, date it and keep a copy, so you can later prove you did it. Below is a form notice you might use. Be sure to keep a **copy** of this notice to use if you later go to court.

Next you must wait a "reasonable time" to give the landlord a chance to make the repairs. After a reasonable time runs out, you can do the repairs. What is a "reasonable time" will depend on the circumstances. If the heat doesn't work in January, a reasonable wait may mean only a few days, at most. If it breaks down in

NOTICE TO REPAIR

To _____ , Landlord of the premises
located at _____ .

NOTICE IS HEREBY GIVEN that unless certain dilapidations on said premises are repaired within a reasonable time, the undersigned tenant shall exercise any or all rights accruing to him pursuant to law, including those granted by California Civil Code Section 1942.

Said dilapidations are the following:

_____

_____

_____

Dated: _____

_____
(signature of tenant)

June, and it is expensive to repair quickly, you should wait a little longer. If you have complained to the landlord about the defect before, then you should not have to wait too long. The law says that 30 days is "presumed" to be a reasonable time. This means that if you do not wait 30 days, if the case goes to court, **you** must prove the wait was reasonable. If you wait 30 days, the landlord must prove the wait was unreasonable.

If the landlord has not made the repairs after a reasonable time, you may do the repairs or hire someone to do them. Keep a record of al time you put in and all amounts you spend on labor and materials.

When the next month's rent is due, give the landlord a written statement itemizing the expenses of the repairs, including compensation for your time. If this adds up to less than the rent, you must pay him the balance.

Remember, you cannot deduct more than one month's rent with your repair and deduct remedy.

c. Retaliation for using Repair and Deduct Remedy

If you have a month-to-month rental agreement instead of a lease, the landlord might try to retaliate against you by giving you a 30-day notice terminating your tenancy or raising your rent.* The problems this raises are discussed on page 80 above. In addition, there are some special restrictions on the tenant's right to stop retaliations against using the repair and deduct remedy (C.C. 1942.5):

- The tenant is protected only for 60 days after he gives the notice of the defects. After that, the landlord can terminate the tenancy or raise the rent, even if the tenant can prove that the landlord is doing it to retaliate.

- The tenant can raise the defense of retaliatory eviction in

---

*He cannot do this if he has agreed to the Model Month-to-Month Rental Agreement discussed in Chapter 2, Part B, of the Handbook, because of paragraph 16.

an eviction law suit only if he is paid up in his rent when he raises the defense.

- The tenant can raise the defense in an eviction lawsuit only if he has not raised this defense in another eviction action brought by the same landlord in the past 12 months.

4. SUE THE LANDLORD

Where the landlord has failed to make repairs which result in a breach of the implied warranty of habitability (discussed on page 74) and you haven't withheld your rent, you may sue your landlord to get back some (or even all) of the rent you paid while the landlord was in breach of the warranty.* In many cases this will be less than $750 and you should consider bringing your suit in Small Claims Court.

5. MOVE OUT

As a last resort, you might simply move out. Under the law, if the landlord's failure to do his duty substantially interferes with your ability to use and enjoy the premises, you can move out in the middle of your lease or rental agreement, without first notifying him that you are doing so. What is "substantial interference" depends on the circumstances. A few cockroaches which come in when it rains might not be, but constant rat infestation would be. You will not be held responsible for any further rent.

This is called the doctrine of "constructive eviction." After you move out, you can also sue the landlord for money damages. You'll need to see a lawyer about pursuing such a suit (see Chapter 1, Part C).

---

*Quevedo v. Braga, 72 Cal. App. 3d Supp. 1 (1977).

TIONAL

VING

If you decide to move out, send the landlord a written notice, such as the one below, and keep a copy for your files.

1500 Acorn Street, #4
Cloverdale, California
March 19, 1977

Smith Realty Co.
10 Jones Street
Cloverdale, California

Dear Sirs:

I reside in apartment #4 at 1500 Acorn Street and regularly pay rent to your office.

As you know, on March 11, 1977 the water heater in my unit broke down. Although I have repeatedly requested repairs, no action has yet been taken. Because of the weather and because of the size of my family, I cannot continue to live comfortably without such an essential service, so I am therefore compelled to exercise my rights under Civil Code Section 1942 to vacate the premises.

If repairs are not made by March 24, 1977 I will vacate the premises and seek whatever other remedies I am entitled to under law.

Very truly yours,

Patricia Parker

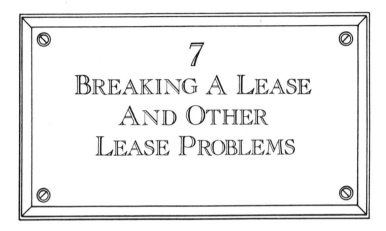

7
BREAKING A LEASE
AND OTHER
LEASE PROBLEMS

A. WHAT HAPPENS WHEN
THE LEASE RUNS OUT

Often a tenant wishes to stay in a dwelling after a lease term expires. If you are in this situation, read your lease carefully as it may have a provision covering this situation. If so, the terms of the lease control unless they call for an illegal automatic renewal (see next paragraph). In the absense of a lease provision, California law states that a tenant who holds over after a lease runs out becomes a month-to-month tenant under the same terms as are in the old lease. All the terms of the original lease, with the exception of the period of occupancy clause, are still binding and become what is, in effect, a written rental agreement (see Chapter 2, Part B). This means that either the landlord or the tenant can terminate the tenancy with a 30-day written notice, likewise, the rent can be increased after a 30-day notice.

Sometimes a lease will contain a provision calling for the automatic renewal of the lease if the tenant stays beyond the end of the lease term. This would mean that if a tenant held over one day after a one year lease expired, he would have renewed the lease for another year. This sort of provision is legal only if the renewal or extension provision is printed in at least eight point boldface type immediately above the place where the tenant signs the lease. If a renewal provision is not set forth in this way it is voidable by the tenant.*

B. HOW TO SUBLEASE

A sublease is what happens when you lease or rent your place to someone else, and you move out and they move in. The subtenant pays an agreed-upon rent to you (it can be more or less than the amount you pay) and you pay rent to the landlord. Sometimes it is possible to have the subtenant pay directly to the landlord. When you sublease you become, in a real sense, a landlord, and must start thinking like one, at least in regard to collecting rent and protecting the condition of the premises. When you sublease, you are still reponsible for all of the terms and conditions of your own lease to the landlord. This means that if your subtenant doesn't pay up or if he wrecks the place, you will be liable to the landlord.

Technically speaking, you are only entitled to sublease when you have a lease yourself in the first place, and if the lease does not prohibit subleasing (although most of them do). Further, a sublease can't be made for a period that extends beyond the end of the original lease. If you have a lease for one year and only seven months remain under it, then, technically, the longest time you can sublease the place is seven months.

As a matter of practice, subleases are often made for periods of time in excess of the original lease. Often, in fact, people with no lease at all will "sublease" their place for a few months while they are on vacation, or the like. This is not, technically, speaking, a valid sublease, and while it may work in practice, if something

*Civil Code section 1945.5.

SUBLEASE AGREEMENT

This is an agreement between Patricia Parker of 1500 Acorn Street #4, Cloverdale, California and Joan Ehrman now residing at 77 Wheat Avenue, Berkeley, California.

1. In consideration of $200 per month payable on the first day of each month Patricia Parker agrees to sublease apartment #4 at 1500 Acorn Street, Cloverdale, California to Joan Ehrman from August 1, 1977 to December 30, 1977.

2. Patricia Parker hereby acknowledges receipt of $500 which represents payment of the first and last months' rent and a $100 cleaning and damage deposit.* The $100 cleaning and damage deposit will be returned to Joan Ehrman on December 30, 1977 if the premises are completely clean and have suffered no damage.

3. A copy of the agreement between Smith Realty and Patricia Parker is stapled to this agreement and is incorporated as if set out in full. Joan Ehrman specifically covenants and agrees to adhere to all the rules and regulations set out in sections 1-10 of this lease.

_____   _____
Date   Patricia Parker

_____   _____
Date   Joan Ehrman

---

*The rules which limit the amount of money that a landlord can charge a tenant for deposits also apply to sub-lease agreements. See p. 34.

goes wrong, you may find yourself over a barrel.

Whenever you let anyone move into your place for a while, it is important to have a written agreement which sets out all the terms of the arrangement. We include here an example of a possible sublease agreement with the warning that it will have to be modified to suit your individual circumstances.

C. HOW TO BREAK A LEASE

1. GENERAL RULES

Often a tenant wants to move before the lease runs out. This need not be a great problem. The same shortage of housing that gives the landlord an advantage at the time of the original rental also makes it possible* for a tenant to get out of a lease fairly easily. When you sign a lease you sign a contract by which you promise to pay rent on certain premises for a certain time (see Chapter 2, Part B). Simply moving out does not get you off the hook as far as paying is concerned. You have made a contract and legally you are bound to fulfill it. This means that you are legally bound to pay rent for the full lease term whether or not you continue to occupy the dwelling. If you do not pay, your landlord can sue you, get a judgment and try to collect the money by doing such things as attaching your wages, either now or in the future.

Indeed, the picture for a tenant breaking a lease would be very bleak were it not for the legal doctrine of contract law that the landlord must take all reasonable steps to keep his damages to a minimum. This means that when the tenant leaves in the middle of the lease term, the landlord must make all reasonable efforts to rent the premises to another tenant at the best price possible. The amount of money, if any, that the landlord can recover from the original tenant is the difference between what the tenant was obligated to pay the landlord under the terms of the lease and what the landlord can get by leasing the premises to someone else for the same period of time. Because of a general shortage of rental units in most areas of California the landlord should be able to get a new tenant fairly quickly for about the same rental as paid by the original tenant. The result is that the tenant who breaks the lease is obligated for little or no damages.**

2. SELF-PROTECTION WHEN BREAKING A LEASE

Notify your landlord in writing as soon as you know that you are going to move before the end of a lease term. The more notice

---

*Civil Code section 1951.2.

WARNING! If your lease contains a clause that says that you have the right to sublease or assign (transfer) the lease, either with or without the landlord's permission, you must be careful. Civil Code section 1951.4 requires that **you find a suitable tenant to take your place in this situation. If you fail to do this, your landlord may be able to sit on his hands and let your rent pile up with no duty to re-rent the place himself (mitigate damages). The law is confused in this area, but to be on the safe side you should find a new tenant, or if the landlord is being difficult, tenants, to take your place.

1500 Acorn Street #4
Cloverdale, California
September 15, 1977

Smith Realty Co.
10 Jones Street
Cloverdale, California

Dear Sirs:

As you know, I occupy unit #4 of your building at
1500 Acorn Street under a lease that runs from June 1, 1977
until May 31, 1978.

Due to circumstances beyond my control it is
necessary for me to move on October 31, 1977. As I paid
my last months' rent when I moved in I will make no rent
payment on October 1, 1977 and will ask that you apply
my last months' rent to the month of October.

I apologize for any trouble I may put you to by
moving out before the end of my lease term and will
cooperate with you in every way to see that a new tenant
is found promptly. Of course, I will rely on you to mitigate
any damages as much as possible.

Yours truly,

Patricia Parker

you give the landlord the better your chances are that he will find another tenant. Send a letter like the one on page 96.

REMINDER: When you send this notice you have in theory violated your lease contract. Your landlord could try to evict you using a three-day notice (see Chapter 9). This is very unlikely, however, as you will have moved out before the matter gets into court.

After sending the landlord your written notice it is wise to stop by and talk to him. He may have another tenant ready to move in and not be concerned by your moving out. In some cases the landlord will want an amount of money to compensate him for his trouble in re-renting the place. If the amount is small it may be easier to agree to pay rather than to become involved in a dispute. If your landlord has a security and/or cleaning deposit, you might offer to let him keep all or part of these in full settlement of all possible damage claims arising from your leaving in the middle of the lease term. As noted above, since the landlord has a duty to try and re-rent the place ("mitigate damages") and since this is reasonably easy to do, you should not agree to pay much in the way of damages. Get any agreement you make in writing.

If it is not possible to deal rationally with your landlord, or if he won't make a written release, you should take steps to protect yourself. Don't let your landlord scare you into paying him a lot of money. Simply put an advertisement in your local paper to lease your dwelling at the same rental that you are paying. When people call, show them the place, but tell them that any lease arrangement must be worked out with your landlord. Give the names of all interested parties to your landlord. Also request that the potential tenants contact the landlord directly. To protect yourself keep a list of all tenants who appear to be suitable and who express an interest in moving in. Include information on your list that indicates that the potential tenants are "responsible," such as job and family. Write a letter to your landlord with a list of the names and keep a copy for your file. He has a right to approve or disapprove of whomever you suggest as a tenant, but he may not be unreasonable about it.

AGREEMENT

This agreement is between Patricia Parker of 1500 Acorn Street #4, Cloverdale, California, and Smith Realty Co., of 10 Jones Street, Cloverdale, California, by its owner, B. R. Smith.

In consideration of the amount of $75, Smith Realty Co. hereby agrees to cancel the lease of Patricia Parker on Apt. #4 at 1500 Acorn Street, Cloverdale, California as of October 31, 1977. The $75 payment is hereby acknowledged to be made this date by cancelling the obligation of Smith Realty Co. to return to Patricia Parker the $75 security deposit paid on June 1, 1977.

_____   _____
Date   B. R. Smith

_____   _____
Date   Patricia Parker

1500 Acorn Street #4
Cloverdale, California
October 1, 1977

Smith Realty Co.
10 Jones Street
Cloverdale, California

Dear Sirs:

As I told you on September 15, 1977, I plan to move out of this apartment on October 31, 1977. Because I wish to keep damages to a minimum I am herewith including the names addresses and phone numbers of four people who have expressed an interest in renting this apartment on or about November 1, 1977 at the same rent that I pay. I assume that you will find one of these potential tenants to be suitable, unless of course you have already arranged to rent the apartment.

(*include list of names and addresses*)

Very truly yours,

Patricia Parker

3. POSSIBLE LEGAL ACTION

After a tenant moves out and breaks a lease he can be sued. This is not likely if the landlord has gotten a new tenant to move in almost immediately after the old tenant moves out, because in such a situation there would be little or no damages. However, occasionally it will take the landlord a little time or expense such as advertising to get a new tenant. In this case he may sue either in Small Claims Court or possibly in Municipal Court.

If you are sued you will have to read the complaint carefully to see if the amount the landlord asks for is fair. As explained above if you take the proper steps to protect yourself he should be entitled to little or nothing. In unusual situations, however, the landlord may be entitled to some recovery. An example of one situation where damages could be recovered would be where a tenant with a year's lease at a $200 per month rental moved out in midyear and no new tenant could be found who would pay more than $175 per month. In this case the old tenant would be liable for the $25 a month difference between what he paid and what the new tenant paid, multiplied by the number of months left in the lease at the time he moved out. A tenant might also be liable for damages if it took the landlord some period of time, such as a month, to find a new tenant. In this case the first tenant would be liable for the month's rent if the landlord had made diligent efforts to find a new tenant.

If you are sued in Small Claims Court for an amount that seems excessive, simply go and tell the judge your side of the case and bring with you any witnesses and written documentation that help tell you story (see page 109). If you are sued in Municipal Court, you will want to see a lawyer, especially if there is a lot of money involved (see Chapter 1, Part C).

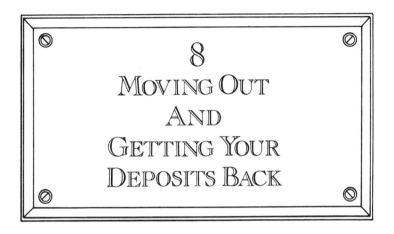

8
MOVING OUT
AND
GETTING YOUR
DEPOSITS BACK

Sooner or later the time comes to move on. Hopefully you are not leaving under fire, but on good terms. Maybe it's just time for some changes. The main concern at this point is with giving notice and getting back deposits which you put up at the outset.

A. GIVING NOTICE

Written notice of your intention to leave should be given in all situations. Oral notice is not legally adequate even if you have an oral rental agreement. Failure to give proper written notice can result in your being obligated to pay an extra month's rent. If you rent under **any** kind of document, read it carefully and see what it says about time and manner of giving notice. If it is silent on the subject, or if you have an oral agreement, then the time for notice is the same as the time between rent payments. If you pay rent once a month, you must give written notice of your moving date 30 days in advance. It is not necessary for your notice of departure to correspond to a due date for rent. That is, it would be proper to pay rent on March 1, give 30 days written notice of intention to move on March 10, and move out on April 9. (Of course, you would be obligated to pay the first 10 days of rent for April on April 1.) **Remember:** Keep a copy of all notices that you send for your file. If you have any reason to distrust your landlord, send the notice by registered or certified mail.

If you rent under a lease, you have made a contract to occupy the premises until the lease runs out. When the lease ends you are free to leave. California law does not require notice at the end of a lease, but **read the provisions of your lease carefully:** you will likely find that it requires you to give a notice in writing 30 days before the lease runs out if you intend to leave, otherwise you will be regarded as automatically switching over to a month-to-month tenancy. This is perfectly legal if called for in the lease and will put you in the same position as if you had a "written rental agreement" as far as giving notice is concerned.

An example of a 30-day notice from the tenant to the landlord appears on the next page.

By the way, don't forget about your deposit of last month's rent. If you paid the last month's rent at the outset, apply it now, and refer to it in your letter.

B. GETTING YOUR DEPOSITS BACK

Be sure to read the discussion on deposits in Chapter 2, Part C.

One of the most common sources of dispute between landlords and tenants is over the return of deposits. Some landlords act as if deposits are part of the rent and try to return them as infrequently as possible. The legal rules are contained in Section 1950.5 of the California Civil Code and are very simple. Within two weeks after the tenant moves out, the landlord must return all cleaning and security deposits or "fees" that are not reasonable necessary to remedy tenant defaults, repair damages caused by the tenant (exclusive of normal wear and tear), or to clean the premises. If the landlord retains any of the tenant's deposits for these purposes, he

1500 Acorn Street #4
Cloverdale, California
April 10, 1977

Smith Realty Co.
10 Jones Street
Cloverdale, California

Dear Sirs:

As you know, I occupy Apartment #4 at 1500 Acorn Street.

This is a formal written notice of my intention to vacate Apartment #4 at 1500 Acorn Street on May 12, 1977. I will, of course, pay you the correct amount of rent on May 1, 1974 to cover the period from May 1 to May 12, 1977.

I plan to leave the apartment clean and in good physical condition and will appreciate the return of my security and cleaning deposit promptly after I move out.

Yours truly,

Patricia Parker

or she must furnish (also within two weeks) the tenant with an itemized written statement of the basis for, and the amount of, any security received and the disposition of such security and shall return any remaining portion of such security to the tenant.

If a landlord acts in **bad faith** and does not return the money or properly account for any part that he keeps, he may be liable for up to $200 in punitive damages over and beyond the amount of the deposits unjustly retained. The burden of proof as the reasonableness of the amounts claimed shall fall on the landlord.

When you are about to move out, if you feel that your apartment has not been damaged beyond normal wear and tear, and if it is clean, you should take the following steps to protect yourself:

- If you filled out a checklist when you moved in as discussed in Chapter 2G (or even if you didn't) it is also a good idea for you and your landlord to fill one out now;

- Just as you did when you moved in, you or a friend should take photographs of the apartment;

- Have some responsible people thoroughly check the dwelling so that they can, if necessary, testify on your behalf that it was clean and in good shape when you moved out;

- Keep as part of your permanent file all receipts for the purchase of cleaning materials that you use in your final clean-up;

- If you rent a waxer or a rug shampooer keep the receipts in your file and have a photograph taken of you using it.

If you are on good terms with your landlord, it makes good sense to invite him over when you get done cleaning to have him go over the place with you. This is the time to discuss particulars about the return of your deposits. If there is any damage, you can discuss a fair price for its repair. You might have already received estimates from repair men to show him.

RENT WITHHOLDING: If your premises are going to be left clean and undamaged, but you anticipate trouble recovering your deposit, there is one common technique available which tenants often employ. Though not technically legal, it can often work as a practical solution. Many people who are planning to move out of the area and will not have easy access to Small Claims Court adopt this technique because they have no other practical way to protect themselves. A month (or more if necessary) before the end of tenancy, add up all deposits, last month's rent, etc. and tell the landlord that you are applying it as rent. He won't be pleased with this approach, but by the time he can get into court you'll be packed up and gone and he will not be entitled to any damages as long as your place was left clean and in good repair. Legally, when you move out the landlord's duty to return the various deposits is set off against your duty to pay rent, so neither party is entitled to damages. It is unlikely that your landlord will take any action, but just in case make sure you have photographs and witnesses to attest to the condition of your place at the time you leave. If you decide to follow this procedure you should clearly explain to your landlord what you are doing in writing (see next page).

In most situations a letter such as this and perhaps a chat with the landlord will clear the matter up. If the landlord gets hostile, however, you may want to deposit the amount of the last month's rent in a trust account at a local bank to be paid to the landlord only after your deposits are returned. The chances of the landlord taking you to court over this issue are very low. If he does, however, your letters and bank account, if you set one up, will be strong indications of your good faith and should be adequate to protect you.

MAKE A FORMAL DEMAND: If you do not use the rent withholding technique discussed above, and if after you vacate you can't get satisfaction from the landlord, you should make a written demand for the return of your money (see page 108).

If the letter doesn't produce results, you can consider seeing an attorney to have him contact the landlord for you. Sometimes his added authority is just right to scare the landlord into a response, and some lawyers are good negotiators. On the other hand, lawyers are expensive—make sure ahead of time exactly what the lawyer will do and how much it will cost.

SUE THE LANDLORD IN SMALL CLAIMS COURT: If the formal demand doesn't work, you should consider suing the landlord. If you rent under a lease or rental agreement which provides for the landlord's attorney's fees, then you, too, are entitled to attorney's fees if you win your law suit. In such situations you might ask an attorney to handle the matter for you. Be sure you thoroughly discuss his fee arrangements ahead of time.

In most cases, however, you should probably bring your own suit in Small Claims Court. The rules governing Small Claims proceedings are contained in the California Code of Civil Procedure, Section 117a-r. The cost for filing papers and serving the landlord will not exceed $6.00.

To sue your landlord in Small Claims Court, go to your local

1500 Acorn Street #4
Cloverdale, California
March 28, 1977

Smith Realty Co.
10 Jones Street
Cloverdale, California

Dear Sirs:

As you know I occupy Apartment #4 at 1500 Acorn Street and regularly pay rent to your office once a month.

Please take note that this is a formal written notice of my intention to vacate apartment #4 on May 1, 1977.

In speaking to other tenants in this area I have learned that from time to time the return of cleaning deposits has been the subject of dispute between landlord and tenant. Accordingly I have decided on the following course of action: Instead of sending you the normal $200 rent payment today, I am sending you instead $50 and ask that you apply the $150 cleaning deposit to my last month's rent.

I will leave the apartment spotless. If you should doubt this or want to discuss this matter further please give me a call and come over. I think that you will be satisfied taht I am dealing with you honestly and in good faith and that the apartment, which is clean now, will be spotless when I leave.

Very truly yours,

Patricia Parker

1500 Acorn Street #4
Cloverdale, California
October 15, 1977

Smith Realty Co.
10 Jones Street
Cloverdale, California

Dear Sirs:

As you know, until September 30, 1977, I resided in apartment #4 at 1500 Acorn Street and regularly paid my rent to your office. When I moved out I left the unit cleaner than it was when I moved in.

As of today I have received neither my $100 cleaning deposit nor my $100 security deposit, nor have I received any accounting from you for that money. Please be aware that I know about my rights under California Civil Code Sect. 1951.5 , and that if I do not receive my money within the next week, I will regard the retention of these deposits as showing bad faith on your part and shall sue you not only for the $200 in deposits, but for the $200 punitive damages allowed in Sect. 1951.5 of the California Civil Code.

May I hear from you soon.

Very truly yours,

Patricia Parker

courthouse and find the Clerk of the Small Claims Court. Tell the Clerk you want to sue your landlord and she will give you a form "affidavit" to fill out. The Clerk is required by law (Code of Civil Procedure Section 117c) to fill it out for you, if you so request. On the form, you must say how much you are claiming the landlord owes you. This amount cannot exceed $750.* You figure the amount you want to claim by asking for the portion of the deposit the landlord owes you plus, if you have a chance of showing "bad faith," $200 in "punitive damages."** If this adds up to more than $750, then you will either have to waive the excess over $750 or else not use the Small Claims Court. If you have to make this decision, you should consider that you may not easily win the full $200 in punitive damages.

After you file the form with the Clerk, she will send a copy of it to the landlord by registered or certified mail, with an order for him to appear in Court for a trial on the suit at a certain date and time. To find out that date and time, ask the Clerk. That date must be not less than 10 nor more than 30 days after the date of the order to appear, if the landlord lives within the county. If he doesn't live in the county, the date must be not less than 30 nor more than 60 days after the date of the order to appear (Code of Civil Procedure Section 117d).

The trial is very informal. No lawyers are present and there are no formal rules of evidence. There is no jury. When you come to court for your hearing bring the file or envelope with your records. All papers or pictures that you believe help your case should be included. Also bring with you all witnesses who have first-hand information about the facts in dispute. If you do not have any experience with a court you can go down a day or two before and watch a few cases. You will see that it is a very simple procedure.

On the day your case is to be heard, get to the court a little early and check for your courtroom (referred to as a department). Sometimes this information is listed on sheets outside the department. If you are confused, go to the clerk's office and they will see that you get to the correct place. When you arrive in the right department, tell the clerk or bailiff that you are present and sit **down and wait until your case is called. When your turn comes, stand at the large table at the front of the room and tell the judge**

---

*Small claims jurisdiction should be raised considerably. Also legislation should be enacted to set up a landlord-tenant court where disputes of all kinds could be settled cheaply and quickly without recourse to expensive lawyers.

**The California Attorney General has ruled that small claims courts may award these punitive damages. Opinion No. 50 75/82 (May 13, 1976).

clearly what is in dispute.

Do not tell him a great long story as he will get bored and possibly irritated. Remember, the judge hears many cases every day, and he will not be particularly excited about yours. If he gets bored he may stop listening and start thinking about what he is going to eat for lunch. Start your presentation with the problem and then give him **only** directly relevant facts. Be brief and to the point—don't ramble. You may show pictures and documents to the judge. When you are done with your oral presentation tell the judge you have witnesses and ask them to testify. The landlord will also have a chance to tell his side. You can expect it to be very different from yours, but stay cool! When he is done you may ask him questions if you feel that he has not told the truth or if he has left some things out. It is wise not to ask the landlord any questions (cross-examine) unless you are trying to make a specific important point. Often asking the landlord a lot of vague questions just gives him more opportunity to tell his side of the case. It is **especially** important to **not** argue with the landlord or any of his witnesses—just get the facts out.

If you cannot speak English and cannot find a volunteer interpreter or afford to hire an interpreter, the court must appoint one for you.*

EXAMPLE: In a case where a landlord has not returned your cleaning deposit after you have moved out and have asked for it, you might present your case something like this: "Good morning Your Honor, my name is John Smith and I now live at 2330 Jones Street. From January 1, 1978 until January 1, 1979 I lived at 1500 Williams Street in a building owned by the Jefferson Realty Company. When I moved out the Realty Company refused to refund my $150 cleaning deposit even though I left the place spotless. I carefully cleaned the rugs, washed and waxed the kitchen and bathroom floors, washed the inside of the cupboards and washed the windows. Your Honor, I want to show you some pictures that were taken of my apartment the day I moved out.** These were taken by Mrs. Edna Jackson who is here today and will testify. Your Honor, I don't have much else to say except that Mrs. Jackson and Mrs. Lincoln are here to testify." You would then ask each witness to testify in turn. After getting their names and ad-

---

*Gardiana v. Small Claims Court, 130 Cal. Rptr. 675 (1976).

** If you completed a checklist of the condition of the premises you will want to show it to the judge at this time.

dresses in the court record your questioning might go something like this*

QUESTION: Mrs. Jackson, were you familiar with the apartment I occupied at 1500 Williams Street?

ANSWER: Yes.

Q.: Were you there the day I moved out on January 1, 1979?

A.: Yes.

Q.: Did you take these pictures that I showed to the Judge?

A.: Yes.

Q.: How can you tell?

A.: Because I remember taking them, and because my name and the date I took the pictures are on the back just as I wrote them.

Q.: Did you have a chance to examine the conditions of the premises on January 1, 1979?

A.: Yes.

Q.: What was the condition of the premises as far as cleanliness is concerned?

A.: It was very clean.

The above is meant only to be an example to show you that being clear, concise and well prepared is important. In most cases you will find that judges are helpful and considerate and that they will help you if you get bogged down.

---

*Don't forget to ask the judge for the $200 in punitive damages that the law allows if you believe that the landlord acted in bad faith in not returning your deposit. See page 104.

9
EVICTIONS

"Eviction" is the common term for the whole process that takes place when a landlord wants to force a tenant to get out. If the tenant fails to get out when he's told to, then the **only** thing the landlord can do, legally, is to go to court and bring an action called "unlawful detainer."

A. ILLEGAL LANDLORD CONDUCT

The law is clear in California that if a landlord wishes to evict his tenant, he must first go to court, giving the tenant prior notice of the court proceedings. He cannot take the law into his own hands by locking the tenant out, taking the tenant's belongings, taking off doors and windows, cutting off the utilities or any other kind of harrassment.

1. LOCK-OUT

Where the landlord locks you out and/or takes your belongings without first going to court, you should see a lawyer right away (see Chapter 1, Part C). He can sue the landlord for money damages and get you back in.* You should also call the police or district attorney, since these acts are crimes.** Even if the police won't arrest the landlord, they may talk to him. Try very hard to get them to at least make a report on the incident, since this might help in later legal proceedings.

Under a new law enacted in 1976, most tenants who live in "residential hotels" (apartment buildings which are called "hotels") are also protected against lockouts.***

If the landlord removes doors or windows, your lawyer can sue him for money damages,† and the police might arrest him on a charge of malicious mischief.‡

2. UTILITY CUT-OFF

If the landlord cuts off your utilities to get you to move, he's really in trouble. Legal Aid attorneys in California were successful in combatting this practice, and the California legislature, at the urging of the California Housing Coalition, passed Section 789.3 of the Civil Code. This section says that any landlord who causes any utility service (including water, heat, light, electricity, gas, telephone, elevator or refrigeration) to be cut off with the intent to terminate occupancy is liable to the tenant for certain damages. The section covers all utilities whether or not service is paid for by the tenant or landlord. The tenant is entitled to sue the landlord and recover the following damages:

- Actual damages (i.e., meat spoiling in the refrigerator after electricity is turned off);

- One hundred dollars for each day or part thereof the tenant is deprived of utility service;

---

*Jordan v. Talbot, 55 Cal. 2d. 597, 12 Cal. Rptr. 488 (1961).
**Penal Code Section 418: Forcible Entry.
†Farvour v. Geltis, 91 Cal. App. 2d 603, 205 P. 2d 424 (1949).
‡Penal Code Section 594: Malicious Mischief.
***Code of Civil Procedure section 1159 and Civil Code section 1940.

- Reasonable attorney's fees if the tenant is successful in the court action.

If your utilities are cut off, see an attorney immediately!

B. SUMMARY OF EVICTION PROCEDURE [*]

If some unfortunate circumstances have brought you to the point where your landlord is ordering you to move, you need to stay calm and realize that nothing terrible is going to happen to you. While you are not in a desirable situation, it is not the end of the world. More than anything, you need to know your rights and how to exercise them.

When a landlord wants to force a tenant to leave he must follow a very strict legal procedure. The law **requires** him to proceed as follows:

1. He must have a legal reason for asking the tenant to leave. There are several circumstances that allow a landlord to bring an "unlawful detainer" action against a tenant. The most common are:

- Failure to pay rent when due;
- Failure to abide by some part of a lease or rental agreement such as keeping a pet when pets are specifically prohibited;
- Failure to leave a dwelling after the landlord has served a proper notice to vacate (one of the great disasters of California law is that tenants without leases can be given a 30-day notice to leave for any reason, except discrimination, or for no reason at all).

2. He must properly serve the tenant with a legally correct notice (more about this is part D);

---

*The eviction procedure from the landlords point of view is set out in a book called **Landlording**. See the back of this book for more information about this book.

3. He must start and win an unlawful detainer law suit (more about this in part D) in which the tenant:

- gets properly served with court papers,
- has a chance to file a legal response,
- is entitled to a court hearing.

4. He must turn the unlawful detainer judgment over to the sheriff or marshal. At this time he must pay a deposit of $50-$75. If the judgment was in Small Claims Court, it can't go to the Sheriff for at least 20 days. A judgment from a Municipal Court can be turned over immediately after it is rendered.

Five Day Final Warning: The Sheriff has no power to collect money from you, nor can he put you in jail for not paying rent. His job is to move you off the premises after he has been given a valid court order telling him to do so. Before he comes out to do this, he must deliver a final five day warning. He can give it to you personally, or tack it on the door and send another in the mail if no one is at home.

The Move: To say the very least, it would be foolish for you or your property to still be in the dwelling at the end of the five days. At that time, anyone still there will be physically removed and any of your possessions still on the property will be inventoried by the Sheriff and turned over to the landlord. If you are foolish enough or unlucky enough to be around and have all this happen to you, do **not** resist the Sheriff, or your next residence will be provided for free in the County Jail. You are also subject to arrest if you return to the dwelling at any time after the Sheriff puts you out.

5. After the eviction, the tenant can try to get back any stored property and the landlord can try to collect money damages from the tenant (this is discussed in part E).

C. PLANNING WHAT TO DO

If you get a notice to vacate, you should get a cup of wine (or chicken soup, if you prefer), sit down, relax, and think things over. Number one fact of importance is that you have plenty of time to work it out—even if the landlord moves as fast as he can (and he probably won't), the very earliest that the Sheriff can show up is three weeks. Actually, it is very likely to take six weeks or longer. If you or your lawyer approach the case actively and negotiate or go into court, then the process can be slowed down a great deal.

One hard fact that you'll have to face is that unless you can get your landlord to change his mind about wanting you to leave, then eventually he can get you out. This means that no matter what else you do about the eviction, you ought to start looking for somewhere else to live.

When you are faced with an eviction, there are only a limited number of things you can do. You can:

- do nothing—just wait until you find another place, or the Sheriff comes, whichever happens first;
- negotiate with your landlord, either yourself or through your lawyer, to try to find a compromise solution to your problems and his;
- go into court (by yourself or with a lawyer) to make your case (and/or gain more time).

What you actually decide to do depends upon many considerations, including whether or not you have a good case, how easily you can get another place, how vulnerable you are to a money judgment, how much time and money you want to spend on your case and all the circumstances involved in your and your landlord's respective situations.

While you are making your plans, keep in mind that in addition to time it also costs a landlord a lot of money for his lawyer and for Sheriff's fees (the total cost to evict a tenant is often $500-$600). If the landlord wins his unlawful detainer suit he will surely get a judgment against a tenant for damages, but he then must go to the trouble of collecting the money. All of this normally makes a landlord reluctant to plunge into an unlawful detainer action if he can get you to move through persuasion. The high cost in time, trouble and money that the landlord faces gives the tenant considerable leverage for negotiation.

If you don't pay your rent, then normally the landlord will do nothing for a few days except perhaps call you up to ask where the rent payment is. This is your chance to tell him what your situation is and try to work it out. Landlords vary enormously as to how long it takes them to start legal proceedings. This has noth-

118

ing to do with the law, but a lot to do with psychology. Because it is expensive and time consuming to bring a legal action, most landlords hope that they will not have to do it. They hope that you will pay or leave voluntarily. It takes different landlords different lengths of time to come to the reluctant conclusion that the tenant is not going to pay the rent. Generally, the big landlord will move faster because he is used to evictions and knows just what to do, whereas the small landlord has to feel his way along.

If you are being evicted and don't want to leave you would be wise to get some help from a tenants' rights organization or perhaps an attorney. (See Chapter 1, Part C.) Consultation and advice from a lawyer need not be expensive and lawyers can often be helpful in negotiating with a landlord. For your information, and in case you cannot afford an attorney, the next section discusses some of the central technicalities of an eviction law suit and how to represent yourself.

D. REPRESENTING YOURSELF

Representing yourself is sometimes the only sensible alternative in landlord-tenant cases — lawyers cost too much. As we have said, lawyers can be very helpful in many situations such as consultation, advice and negotiation. You will have to decide how much help you need and how much you can pay. But don't despair about representing yourself; thousands of people like you have managed it very well and often report that handling their own affairs has given them a great deal of satisfaction.

1. NEGOTIATING A SETTLEMENT

Negotiating your own settlement is probably the thing that you are most competent to do, but **not** if you and your landlord can't speak to one another reasonably and logically. If he's mad at you, your job will be a hard one! Also, often times the landlord's attorney may think he can intimidate a layman (you'll show him!) whereas he wouldn't be as likely to try this with another lawyer.

If you decide to do your own negotiating, start as soon as possible to communicate with your landlord. Try to understand what his problems are and try to get him to understand yours. Then try to find a compromise solution that will solve both your problems.

The landlord's power lies in his threat to take you to court, get you thrown out and get a judgment against you for a lot of money. Your power lies in the fact that for him to do this costs him time and a lot of money. If the landlord understands your problems and thinks that you are sincerely trying to get out, or if you promise to get out by a certain date, then he would probably want to avoid the expense and hassle of a law suit by making a deal with you. If you have any claim at all to a good defense (see Part 3, below) you have a mighty weapon, for if you go to court with it, you can greatly increase the time of the eviction and expense to the landlord.

The range of possible deals is as wide as the numbers of cases — just try to do the best you can with your circumstances. Landlords have been known to go so far as to pay the tenant a little money to help him move, and forget the due bill, if the tenant will just get out quickly. In many cases such a solution can end up to be much cheaper for him in the long run. However, it would be more typical for the landlord to agree to drop the law suit in exchange for your agreement not to contest his eviction, to get out by a certain date and to pay a certain sum of money, presumably something less than he might otherwise win against you in court.

In some cases the landlord will not want to drop his law suit completely, but he may instead be willing to agree ahead of time to the kind of judgment he will seek.

If you can make a deal, it is absolutely essential that you have it in writing to protect yourself against mistakes and double-dealing. A letter from the landlord or his attorney clearly stating everything that was agreed to in detail is adequate. If you end up having to draw up the agreement yourself, you can use the example below as a guide. Use whichever parts apply to you or make up your own.

2. TECHNICAL INFORMATION

The material in this section is by no means complete. It is mere-

AGREEMENT

PATRICIA PARKER of 1500 Acorn Street, Apartment #4, Cloverdale, California, and SMITH REALTY CO., by their manager and authorized representative B. R. Smith, hereby agree as follows:

PATRICIA PARKER agrees:

(a) not to contest the unlawful detainer action brought against her by SMITH REALTY in Cloverdale Municipal Court;

(b) to leave the premises no later than _____;

(c) to pay to SMITH REALTY the sum of $_____, which sum when paid shall be full satisfaction for any and all obligations to SMITH REALTY, or agents, to date;

(d) etc. . . .

SMITH REALTY agrees:

(a) to drop the unlawful detainer action brought against PATRICIA PARKER in Cloverdale Municipal Court, Action #_____;

(b) to pay to PATRICIA PARKER the sum of $_____ if she vacates the above premises no later than _____, 1977;

(c) to seek judgment against PATRICIA PARKER for no more than $_____, said sum to be inclusive of all damages, attorneys fees and court costs;

(d) etc. . . .

_____   _____
Date   Smith Realty

_____   _____
Date   Patricia Parker

ly a summary of the more important technicalities involved in an eviction proceeding. Reading this section will help you understand eviction better, and give you basic information in the event that you decide to take your own case into court. If you really want to do a thorough job of researching eviction procedures, we strongly urge you to read **California Eviction Defense Manual** by Moskovitz, Honigsberg & Finkelstein. You should be able to find it in your County Law Library.

a. Notice Requirements

In order for a landlord to win an unlawful detainer action to evict a tenant he **must** start by serving the tenant with a written notice. Landlords usually know how to make and serve notices properly. If a landlord does it wrong, your remedy is to raise the defect as a technical basis. You then gain time, as the landlord will have to start all over again. This is a very strong point with which you or your lawyer can bargain for other concessions.

Below is a brief summary of the technical rules regarding notice and service:

i. 3-day notices. If you are late with your rent in any amount, the landlord can serve you with a written notice to either pay up within three days **or** get out. The notice must describe the premises in question and state the amount of rent due. It must give the tenant the choice of paying or leaving. This means that if the tenant pays the amount demanded within three days, then the notice is satisfied and is of no further meaning. Three day notices can also be given for other specific breaches of lease or rental agreements (i.e., loud parties or pets prohibited by the agreement). In each case the notice must specify the fault and demand its correction within three days as an alternative to moving out.

Counting the Three Days: To correctly count the three days, ignore the day on which the notice is served. Start counting with the next day and pay up by the end of the third day. If the third day falls on a Saturday, Sunday or court holiday, you have until the end of the next business day to pay up.

If the landlord accepts any amount of money at all from you after the notice is served he **may possibly** be required to start all over again with a new notice before going to court. The law is unclear on this point, but many municipal court judges have held that a landlord interrupts his own proceedings if he accepts part payments.

CAUTION: It sometimes happens that a three-day notice will be combined with a 30-day notice, all in the same document. In such cases, even if the tenant cures the fault such as paying the past due rent or getting rid of the dog within three days, he will still have to face the demand that he vacate in 30 days. Read the notice carefully.

ii. 30-day Notices. Unless you have a lease for a longer period of time, you can be given a notice to leave in 30 days for any reason whatsoever or for none at all. All 30-day notices must be in writing. If the period between rent payments is shorter than 30 days, then your notice can correspond to the shorter period.

iii. Proper Service of Notices. A three-day notice must be served on you in one of these ways: (1) handed to you personally; or (2) handed to a fairly grown-up child or adult on the premises **and** a copy sent to you by mail; or (3) if no one is home, the notice may be posted in a conspicuous place and a copy sent by mail. A 30-day notice may be served by first class mail.

COMMENT: If you receive a three-day notice, you can comply with the demand to pay rent and that's the end of it. However, if you get a 30-day notice, there's no real choice — if you don't leave, you will have to face the landlord's next action, probably a law suit. You can try to talk your way into staying, but if the landlord is set on getting you out, it is almost impossible to stay in peaceful possession of the premises. However, through negotiations and other strategies, much can still be accomplished. Offer some money — if a landlord accepts money as rent for a time period starting after the thirty day notice runs out, then the notice is nullified and he will have to start over again.

If you can't talk your way into staying, at least try to work out delays, returns of deposits and other concessions from the landlord. Some landlords have found it cheaper to pay tenants some money to move out rather than spend a larger sum on legal action.

If you get a notice, it is time to decide quickly what course of action to take. If you can, see a lawyer for advice.

b. The Law Suit

If, (1) you have been properly served with a three-day or 30-day notice, and (2) when the time is up you are still on the premises, then, and only then, the landlord is eligible to go to court. Once the landlord goes to court, it will be **at least** several weeks and often much longer before the Sheriff actually comes to move you out.

124

The name of the law suit brought to evict a tenant is "unlawful detainer." Landlords will almost always bring this action in the local Municipal Court, but it is possible for it to be done in Small Claims Court **if** your tenancy is not longer than month to month. Small Claims Court is less expensive for the landlord, since no attorneys are involved, but it takes as long as two months or more to get a tenant out. Also, in Small Claims Court damages are limited to $750. There are some important differences in details between the two courts, but the major procedures are similar. In either court you must be properly served with a Summons and Complaint before the action can get under way; then there must be a hearing; and, if you lose, judgment must be entered against you. Following judgment, the matter is taken to the Sheriff for the heavy-handed part.

i. The Landlord's Court Papers. The court action is started when the landlord (or his attorney) files an unlawful detainer "Complaint." The Complaint is a document which briefly states the case against you, asks the court to order you out, and for a judgment against you for a certain amount of money to cover past due rent, attorney's fees, court costs and other damages. It is proper for him to ask for attorney's fees **only** if you rented under a document which has a provision stating that attorney's fees are recoverable. Landlords usually ask for treble damages (three times what you actually owe). They have a legal right to make this request if they claim that the tenant was guilty of malice or bad faith in not leaving sooner. In most cases the judge will use his discretion to limit damages to that amount actually incurred by the landlord unless he feels that the tenant is deliberately trying to use the legal process to harass or cheat the landlord.

When the unlawful detainer complaint is filed, the court automatically issues a Summons. The Summons is a notice from the court telling you that the action has started and how much time you have to respond. In Municipal Court, the Summons will tell you that in order to contest the case you **must** file a written "Answer" within five days of the day you were served, unless you were served by "substituted service" (see D2 below) in which case you have 15 days to file an answer.

ii. Serving the Court Papers. After filing his papers, the landlord **must** serve you with a copy of the Summons and Complaint. In Small Claims Court this can be done by handing them to you or by sending them to you via certified or registered mail. In Municipal Court the rules governing service are a little more strict. Here you must be handed the papers personally or by a procedure known as "substituted service" must be followed. Under this method a tenant who can't be served personally after reasonably diligent effort can be served by leaving a copy of the complaint and summons in the hands of a person at least 18 years old at the tenant's home or business after telling that person what the papers concern. In addition, another copy of the complaint and summons must be mailed to the tenant.

iii. The Tenants Answer. If the action is in Small Claims Court, you do not need to file a written answer in order to be heard—you need only show up at the time of the hearing. However, most unlawful detainer actions are in Municipal Court, and in such cases to get a chance to present your side you must file a formal written "answer" within five days of receipt of the Summons and Complaint. (If the fifth day falls on a Saturday, Sunday or holiday, the answer is due on the next business day.) If "substituted service" was used, you are allowed 15 days in which to answer. In the Answer you deny the errors in the landlord's complaint, and raise your own defenses.

iv. The Court Hearing. There is a court hearing in **every** unlawful detainer case. If the case is uncontested, the landlord says his piece and wins. If there is a contest, the judge listens to both sides, then makes his judgment.

v. The Court Judgment. After the unlawful detainer complaint has been served on you, if you do not respond your landlord will get a default judgment against you. If you or your attorney respond and go to court you may still lose and get a judgment entered against you, but it will take at least several weeks longer. If you go to court and win, the judgment will be entered against your landlord.

c. Outline of an Eviction Law Suit

Here is a brief outline of the main possible procedural steps in an eviction law suit filed in a Municipal Court. Most, if not all, of the steps are too technical for you to handle yourself, but you should know all the possibilities.

The landlord (called the "plaintiff") files his complaint in court. He then has a process-server serve a copy of the complaint and summons on the tenant ("defendant"). Within five days after this, the tenant must file in court, (and serve a copy on the landlord's attorney by mail), one of the following documents: an "answer", which says that the allegations of fact in the complaint are not true; a "demurrer", which says that the complaint is not drawn up correctly in a legal, technical sense; a "motion to strike", which says that some of the allegations or demands for relief in the complaint are improper; or a "motion to quash" the service of summons, which says that the summons was not legally proper or was not served properly.

If a motion to quash is filed, the judge will hold a hearing on it and decide it in a week or two. If the judge grants this motion, the landlord must have the tenant served with process again, essentially starting all over again.

If the motion to quash is denied, the tenant's attorney may then file a demurrer or motion to strike, if there are grounds for one of these. It may take another week or two for the judge to hear and decide this. If a demurrer is sustained or a motion to strike is granted, the landlord's attorney will have to rewrite his complaint. If the demurrer is overruled or the motion to strike is denied, the tenant's attorney will be given a few days to file an answer to the complaint.

The answer may deny some of the allegations of fact in the complaint. It may also raise certain "affirmative defenses", which

127

say that even if the allegations in the complaint are true, there are additional facts which require the court not to evict the tenant. These may involve such things as fraud in making the lease, racial discrimination, retaliatory eviction and breach of the "implied warranty of habitability."

After the answer is filed, the case will be set for trial. Either side may request a jury trial if he puts up a deposit for jury fees (about $72, recoverable from the losing party) or gets the judge to allow him to proceed "in forma pauperis." Otherwise, the judge will hear and decide the facts. The trial will be set for anywhere between a week to a month or so away, depending on how crowded the court calendar is. (Eviction cases have "precedence" over other civil cases.)

Before the trial, either attorney may engage in "discovery"—that is, trying to find out what evidence the other side has to prove their case and what he can get him to admit. This may be done by "written interrogatories" or by a "deposition" at which the other party must come and answer questions under oath. A "motion to produce" may also be used, if you want to look at documents in the other party's possession.

At the trial, the landlord's attorney puts on his case, having witnesses testify as to the facts. The tenant's attorney may cross-examine them. Then the tenant's attorney puts on his witnesses and the landlord's attorney then cross-examines them. Then each attorney makes an argument, and the jury or judge decides the case.

If the landlord wins, the tenant can appeal, but whether he can stay in possession during the appeal is up to the trial court judge, who might well condition such a "stay" on the tenant's paying the rent.

If the tenant wins, he obtains a judgment requiring the landlord to pay his court costs and, if the lease or rental agreement provided for attorney's fees for either side, for attorney's fees.

If the landlord wins, he will receive a "judgment" for (1) unpaid rent or, if the tenant refused in "bad faith" to pay rent or get out, up to three times the unpaid rent, (2) his court costs, (3) his attorney's fees, if the lease or rental agreement so provided, and (4) a

128

"writ of restitution" for the premises.

If the tenant failed to file an answer on time, the landlord would obtain a "default judgment" containing all of these things without the tenant having a chance for a trial (unless the tenant quickly filed and was granted a "motion to set aside" the default and default judgment).

The landlord takes his judgment to the civil division of the county sheriff's office. If he deposits certain sheriff's fees (which are added to the judgment), the sheriff will "execute" the money part of the judgment by attaching the tenant's wages or bank account. He will execute the writ of restitution by serving a "notice to vacate" on the tenant. This requires the tenant to move out in five days. If he does not, the sheriff will come out and physically evict him.

All of these procedural devices are more fully explained in the **California Eviction Defense Manual** (available in your County Law Library), which also contains forms for using them.

3. DEFENDING YOURSELF

In the second part of this section we discuss how to defend yourself in Small Claims Court. However, as we've already said, most unlawful detainer suits are filed in Municipal Courts, so the major part of our attention is there.

a. In Municipal Court

Defending yourself in a municipal court can be complicated. Eviction law suits are very technical and difficult for a non-lawyer to defend. Also, some judges simply do not give laymen (especially low-income people) the respect that they give lawyers. Similarly, the landlord's lawyer will be more likely to make a "deal" favorable to you with your lawyer rather than you, since he believes that a lawyer will be better able to defeat or delay the eviction suit. It is a sad commentary on our laws that it is so hard for ordinary folks to speak for themselves, especially if you consider that this condition is not really necessary.*

---

*Most, if not all eviction actions could and should be taken out of Municipal Court and assigned to a "landlord-tenant" court. This would involve simplifying many archaic procedural rules and reducing the need for lawyers.

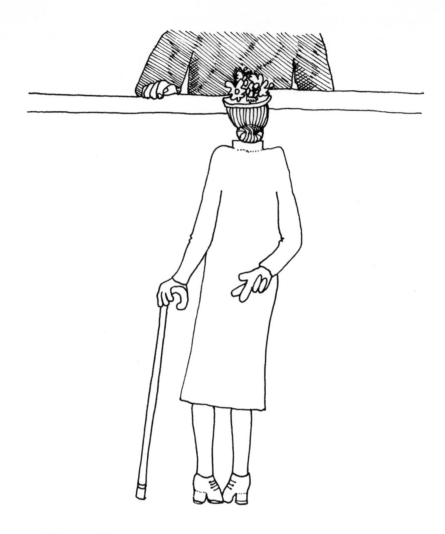

If you still want to go ahead and represent yourself, it is your right to do so. Many others have managed it very successfully. We are only going to show you how to file a simple answer which will get you into court. You may have other remedies, but they are beyond the scope of this book. If you desire to defend your case in a more sophisticated manner, making legal motions and raising affirmative defenses, go to a law library and ask to see the **Califor-**

nia Eviction Defense Manual by Moskovitz, et al. This book contains information and authorities on the various procedures and defenses, with copies of the relevant statutes and useful forms.

Your answer must be filed within five days after you are served with court papers (if the fifth day falls on a weekend or holiday, file it on the next business day).

The answer should be typed (original and three copies) on numbered legal-type paper (available at any stationery store). It should be made like the illustration on the following pages.

It is important that the Answer be signed by **all** of the named defendants. The Verification need only be signed by any one defendant. The "Declaration of Service by Mail" must be signed by someone who is **not** a defendant and who is a citizen over the age of 18.

After you prepare your Answer and Declaration, have one copy mailed to the landlord's lawyer (or, if he has none, to the landlord) and keep the other copies. Take the original to the office of the Clerk of the court in which the complaint was filed. To file it, you will have to pay a filing fee. How much this is depends on how many defendants there are. It will probably be between $10 and $25, payable by cash or money order only.

A few days after you file your answer, you will probably receive a notice from the clerk of the court telling you when the trial will be. On the day of the trial, make sure you show up on time, ready to prove your case, **with any witnesses you have.** (Letters or other documents will probably not be accepted unless they are from the landlord or his agent. You must have "live testimony.")

When you get to the trial, here are some of the possible defenses you might raise, if they fit your case and if you can prove them:

1. In cases where the Complaint is based on a three-day notice:

- you did not get one;
- notice failed to specify the correct amount of rent overdue;

[text continued on page 135]

1 Your name _____
2   Address _____
3   _____
4   Phone _____
5 Defendant, in pro per
6
7
8
9   MUNICIPAL COURT OF THE STATE OF CALIFORNIA
10   _____
11
12   _____,
13   Plaintiff(s)   No. _____
14   vs.
15   _____,   ANSWER
16   Defendant(s)
17
18   Defendant(s) answer the complaint as follows:
19
20   I
21   Admit the allegations contained in paragraph(s)_____ , _____ ,
22 and _____ [of the 1st Cause of Action, and paragraph(s) _____ ,
23 _____ and _____ of the 2d Cause of Action].
24
25   II
26   With the exception of the admisisons set forth above, defendant(s) deny
27 each and every, all and singular, generally and specifically the allegations
28 contained in paragraph(s) _____ , _____ and _____ [of the 1st Cause
29 of Action, and paragraphs _____ , _____ and _____ of the 2d Cause
30 of Action].
31
32   WHEREFORE Defendant(s) pray that Plaintiff(s) take nothing by this

action; that defendant(s) recover costs of suit including reasonable attorneys fees; and for such other relief as may be deemed just.

⑥ ———————⟶ _____
                              Defendant

                         _____
                              Defendant

VERIFICATION

I am (a) defendant in the above action; I have read the foregoing Answer, and know the contents thereof; and I certify that the same is true of my own knowledge.

I certify, under penalty of perjury, that the foregoing is true and correct.

Executed on _____ *[date]* _____, 197__, at _____ *[place]* _____, California.

⑦ ———————⟶ _____
                              Defendant

PROOF OF SERVICE BY MAIL

I am a citizen of the United States and a resident of the county of _____, I am over the age of 18 years and not a party to the above action; my residence address is: _____, California. On_____, 197__, I served the within Answer on the Plaintiffs in said action by placing a true copy thereof enclosed in a sealed envelope with postage thereon fully prepaid, in the United States post office mail box at_____ *[city]* _____, California, addressed as follows: **⑧**

_____

I, _____ *[name of sender]* _____, certify under penalty of perjury that the foregoing is true and correct. Executed on _____ *[date]* _____, 197__, at_____ *[city]*, California.

⑨ ———————⟶ _____
                              [signature]

- notice failed to give you the alternative of paying up (or stop violating lease) **or** getting out;
- notice did not state "clearly and unequivocally" that you are to get out if you don't pay up or quit violating lease;
- notice served on you before rent actually due;
- the amount of rent demanded was incorrect because you agreed on a different rent with the landlord;
- the complaint was served on you before the three days (from the date of service of the three-day notice) ran out;
- although the complaint says you violated the lease or rental agreement, it did not tell you which provision;
- the landlord accepted rent after giving you the three-day notice.

2. In cases where the complaint is based on a 30-day notice:

- you did not get one;
- the 30-day notice did not "clearly and unequivocally" tell you to get out at the end of 30 days;
- the complaint was filed before the 30 days ran out;
- the landlord accepted rent for a period of time beyond the 30-day notice.

3. Other defenses:

- although the complaint asks for "treble damages" because you allegedly refused to move "in bad faith" or "willfully held over," you had good reasons for being unable or unwilling to move;

   NOTE: Since most complaints ask for treble damages, this defense is your most certain justification for filing an Answer and going to court. Even if you have no other valid defense, it is reasonable to go to court to try to avoid treble damages (and, in the process, you get more time before the Sheriff comes).

- the landlord is trying to evict you because of your race;
- the landlord is trying to evict you in retaliation for your reporting code violations to a city agency, for organizing other tenants, for legally withholding rent, or for using your "repair-and-deduct" remedy;
- the landlord materially breached his "implied warranty of habitability" (see section on rent withholding in Chapter 6) *

---

* Here is a way your answer might raise this issue: After you deny the landlord's statements as discussed on pages 132-134 and before the paragraph entitle WHEREFORE, type:

Affirmative Defense - Breach of
Implied Warranty of Hability

I

Defendant admits that he failed to pay the amounts of rent alleged in the complaint to have been due. Defendant alleges, however, that said rent was not due and owing, because during the period for which rent was allegedly due, plaintiff was in violation of the implied warranty of habitability.

ly comply with the rules before he can evict you.*

If you have any questions or problems with preparing your answer or with other court procedures, go see the Clerk of the court. Clerks are sometimes quite helpful (and sometimes they're not!).

b. Small Claims Court

Many landlords prefer to bring their eviction law suits in Small Claims Court, rather than regular municipal court. Since the procedures are easier, the landlord can handle the case himself and save the expense of hiring a lawyer. Since lawyers are not allowed in Small Claims Court, the landlord doesn't have to worry about the tenant having a lawyer to fight for him. However, while an attorney cannot represent you in Small Claims Court, he can advise your on how to represent yourself.

If you want to look them up, the rules regarding Small Claims Court are mostly contained in the California Code of Civil Procedure, Sections 117a through 117r.

II

During such period, plaintiff was required by law to substantially comply with certain housing code provisions, but failed to do so, in the following respects: Now specify each defect. For example: The toilet constantly leaked water onto the bathroom floor, and the premises have been infested with cockroaches.

III

Plaintiff had knowledge of said conditions and a reasonable time to correct them, but he failed to do so.

IV

Said defective conditions were not caused by the wrongful conduct or abnormal use of the premises by defendant or any person under his authority.

V

Because of said defective conditions, the reasonable rent for the period for which plaintiff is claiming rent due is zero. Therefore, plaintiff is entitled to no rent whatsoever and is not entitled to evict for nonpayment of said rent.

*Horton-Howard v. Payton, 44 Cal. App. 108, 112, 186 Pac. 167 (1919).

136

The landlord can use Small Claims Court to evict you only if (1) the term of your tenancy is no longer than month-to-month and (2) the amount of rent or damages he claims does not exceed $750.

The landlord begins his law suit in Small Claims Court by filing an "affidavit" which sets out what he is alleging and demanding. The Clerk of the court then mails a copy of this to the tenant, with an order setting the date and time for trial, which will usually be 10 to 30 days later.

At the trial, the landlord presents his case and then you present your case. You and your witnesses testify under oath. Formal rules of evidence do not apply. Nevertheless, you should be prepared to present your case persuasively, smoothly and quickly. Small Claims Court judges are usually able to allow only a few minutes for each case. Do **NOT** try to argue with the landlord or his witnesses. Be cool and just present your own side as clearly as you can.

For possible defenses to raise, look at the list in the above section.

After the trial, the judge will usually take the case "under submission," and will notify the parties of his decision in a few days by postcard.

If the landlord loses, he cannot appeal. He is all through. If he still wishes to evict you, he will have to find new grounds for doing so.

If the landlord wins, he will receive a judgment like the one he would get in regular municipal court, except that the money part cannot exceed $750. The judgment **cannot** be turned over to the Sheriff during the 20 days after judgment is entered. During this time, you may file a **notice of appeal** to the Superior Court. If you file a notice of appeal during this period, the case is transferred to the Superior Court, where you will recieve a brand new trial (a "trial de novo") and may have an attorney. Until that trial, execution of the judgment against you is automatically stayed (C.C.P. Section 117j).

Note that, unlike the appeal from a regular municipal court judgment, where a stay of execution is in the "discretion" of the trial court judge, this stay is automatic, and no bond or other conditions can be placed on the stay. For this reason, the fact that the landlord uses the Small Claims Court **can** be more useful to **you** than to him. If you win there, you win, and if you lose there, you get a new chance in Superior Court, and the landlord loses a lot of time. You get this, however, only if you file your notice of appeal on time. Therefore, **if you lose a Small Claims Court case, see an attorney right away**, so he can file the notice of appeal and represent you in the new trial in Superior Court.

If the tenant loses in Superior Court, an attorney's fee of $15 will be added to the judgment against him, and the judgment may then be executed.

E. AFTER THE EVICTION

1. THE LANDLORD CAN TRY TO COLLECT MONEY DAMAGES

The landlord's judgment will almost certainly include an award for a sum of money. Once he gets you out, he can try to collect this money. He can garnish your wages if you work, or he can go after your bank account of any valuable property you have which is not covered by California exemption laws.* If the Sheriff or Marshal locked up any of your property when he moved you out, the landlord can definitely **not** satisfy his judgment out of this property.

2. YOU CAN TRY TO GET YOUR PROPERTY BACK

When the Sheriff or Marshall inventories your property, it is then turned over to the landlord. Usually, he will put it into storage. The landlord must hold the property for at least 30 days before putting it up for sale. During this time, you can redeem your property simply by paying storage costs. Even if the property is lawfully sold, the landlord still may not keep any amount above the storage costs. You are entitled to the rest. If the landlord violates the rules, you should see a lawyer, or consider suing him in Small Claims Court.

---

*If you are having debt problems we recommend **California Debtors' Handbook - Billpayers' Rights,** Warner and Honigsberg, Nolo Press. See advertisement at back of this book.

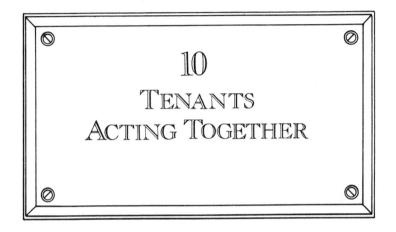

10
TENANTS
ACTING TOGETHER

So far in this book all of the solutions to tenants' problems have been discussed for the tenant acting alone. Acting alone is not nearly as likely to produce results as is acting together with other people, but people on their own resources is the rule these days rather than the exception. This chapter is about methods and techniques by which tenants can gather themselves together and organize to deal with the landlord and with law makers, but all the organization in the world is not worth one bit of neighborliness— and the organization is not nearly as likely to succeed without it.

In many places in California it feels like people have forgotten what "neighbor" means, and how to be good neighbors to one another. Neighborliness is based upon caring, understanding and need. If you have caring and understanding in your heart, you don't need any of this mundane advice anyway. What about needs? If an intruder is sneaking into your place and you yell for help, it would be good if someone came running. If Mrs. Jones next door is sick, maybe you could take her some soup or help

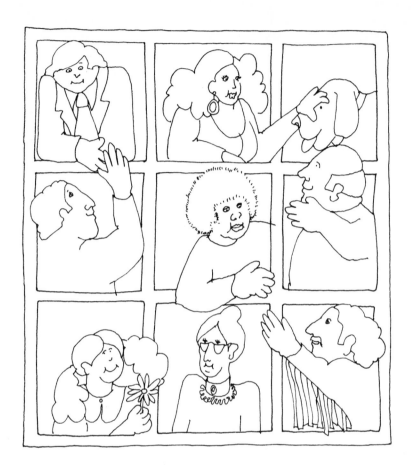

with the kids—who knows when you will need the favor returned? And favors are not always returned by the same people who owe you, but what matter, so long as the accounts roughly balance? Help her. If your washer breaks, maybe someone in the block knows how to fix it, and maybe they'd like some of your famous pie! If all you local folks get together you can have fun. You can take turns taking all the kids to a ball game or have a picnic. You can buy food at wholesale every other week and distribute it. And woe to the landlord who tries to mess with anyone in a unit full of people that get along together and who have read this book!

140

Do the people in your neighborhood look like you? Are "they" your age? Do "they" dress like you? Talk about the same things? See the world the same way? Pray the same way? Who cares— "they" are your neighbors. You need them, they need you and you can all help each other and have a good time to boot. If you think that you can pick the people in your life the same way you choose which channel to put on the T.V., you are mistaken. You get the ones that live around you, whoever they are, and you can't turn off the ones that aren't easy to deal with. You have to learn, grow and take risks. That's why so many folks prefer T.V. to people —T.V. is more predictable, easier to get along with, more reliable and you can control it. But it doesn't care about you, it won't help you when the cards are down, it isn't real and it isn't satisfying. So turn it off and get out into your apartment building and your block and confront your immediate environment. Make friends with it. Get past fear and learn the excitement of diversity. Chat a little, have a drink or a smoke together, help one another if you can, and when the landlord messes with you the next time, boy! will he get a surprise!

A. TENANT ORGANIZING

As we have seen, the odds in favor of an individual tenant getting an unreasonable landlord to be more reasonable are low. The landlord has most of the power. Not only is state law heavily weighted in his favor, but he normally has far more in the way of financial resources than does the tenant. Most landlords can afford attorneys—most tenants cannot. As long as tenants are divided he can deal with each one separately and will almost always come out on top.

In many ways the landlord/tenant situation in **1978** is similar to the labor/management situation of 1900. At the turn of the century one worker without a union had little chance of getting better working conditions or wages from a giant corporation. Indeed, a worker who showed the bad sense to make such a request would probably be walking the bricks in a big hurry. While one tenant dealing with a small landlord **may** be able to work out a sensible relationship as neither party has a great deal more power than the other, the individual tenant dealing with the large landlord has little real chance of influencing his situation very much. In fact, he is in much the same situation as was the worker before unions came on the scene. The bigger the business, the more it is run like a machine, the more humanity is forced out. The tenant either conforms to the hundreds of rules in the lease and lets his rent be raised whenever it suits the landlord, or he is out on the street trying to find another place that will probably be just as bad. This is supposed to be a "free country." Pity the poor tenant who is given life by God and freedom by the United States Constitution, only to have most of it impaired by the standard form lease. Of what value is all your freedom if the only place you can find to live will not let you have a pet, a baby, a party or hang a picture on the wall. As one tenant remarked recently, "The only thing I can do in my apartment is sleep—and if I snore, I'm in trouble."

There is a way to restore the balance of power in landlord/tenant relationships, at least to some degree. It involves getting tenants together and bargaining with the landlord as a group.

A tenant union begins as a group of tenants who want to change their relationship with their landlord. This can involve forcing him to make repairs, stopping a rent increase, or stopping arbitrary treatment of tenants. The tenant union may fight the landlord and force him to sign an agreement—called a collective bargaining agreement—giving the tenants all or some of what they demand. If the tenant union is together enough, it will also force the landlord to deal with the union on a continuing basis.

To understand why a tenants' organization can work, consider the material in Chapter 1, Part B. As we discussed there, the landlord business normally operates so that the landlord has very little of his own cash tied up in the building or buildings that he claims to own. Most of the time he is simply taking money from tenants in the form of rent, giving it to the bank in the form of mortgage payments and the City in the form of taxes, and pocketing the difference. To pay his bills the landlord is dependent upon the majority of his tenants paying the rent. While he can easily deal with a few tenants who hassle him, he is not equipped to handle any sort of concerted tenant action. If all of a sudden no one pays the rent he is in real trouble. He can, of course, bring an "unlawful detainer" against every tenant, but this is extremely expensive. In the meantime, he is getting no rent for a considerable period of time and his bills are piling up.

Just as to a labor union the ultimate weapon is the ability to strike, so, too, the strike is the ultimate sanction possessed by a tenants organization. This does **not** mean, however, that the strike should be used often. Many labor unions rarely strike. They don't need to. They are well organized and are able to negotiate from strength. Sensible management will normally accept the fact that people have gotten together and be willing to negotiate a livable contract. Tenants, like union members, should work to create a sound, well supported organization that can negotiate from strength and which seeks to arrive at understanding rather than conflict.

Tenant unions are usually set up in a crisis situation, when some dispute arises. This is not always the case, however. Even when no dispute is going on, a tenant union can be a good organization for neighbors to get together to organize social activities, baby-sitting cooperatives, wholesale food purchases and the like, as well as to establish a group to deal with the landlord when problems arise.

This chapter will give you some ideas on how to set up a tenant union, tactics to use in pressuring the landlord, and how to negotiate a good agreement with him. Keep in mind, however, that **a tenant union is only as effective as the will of its members and leaders to make it effective.** This takes time, energy, patience, and the willingness to take risks. Most of all, it takes a sense of community, understanding and identity between the tenants. Knowing techniques may be helpful, but it cannot replace these essential qualities. If you feel that these qualities are not there and cannot be inspired, you probably should give up the idea of forming a tenant union. Read the opening paragraphs of this chapter one more time, then find some way of dealing with the landlord by yourself.

There are several organizations in California actively organizing and giving advice to tenants.

Unfortunately, because of lack of funding, tenants' rights groups have a hard time sustaining themselves. In the past we have tried to print a list of local organizations here, but because groups come and go so fast this is no longer practical. You should be able to get accurate, up-to-date information as to whether a tenants' organization exists in your area from California Housing Action and Information Network (CHAIN), P. O Box 2103, Sacramento, California 95810.

B. SETTING UP A TENANT'S UNION

1. GET THE TENANTS TOGETHER AT A MEETING

Two or three concerned tenants can start a tenant's union, if they are willing to do the work.

First, set a meeting time and place. Both should be convenient for most of the tenants.

Next, contact the tenants and ask them to come to the meeting. If you can possibly afford the time, do this in person, door-to-door. Recruit other tenants to help you. Use posting or distribution of notices only as a last resort or as a supplement to personal contact. If there are different races or ethnic groups in the building, try to get someone from each group to do the initial contacting of his own people.

2. THE FIRST MEETING

The first meeting should be conducted informally. People should get to know each other. They should be encouraged to speak about problems they have had with the building or the landlord. This way they will see what problems they have in common.

After this, explain to people the possibilities of collective action. Through reading this Handbook, you have seen how the law and the "market-place" are stacked against the tenant if he tries to deal with the landlord **individually,** but effective use of tactics described in this chapter can get greater gains **if the tenants act as a group**. Explain some of these tactics to them and use the labor union analogy. Explain that the tenants can also work out child care, whoesale food purchases, parties and the like, if they can learn to act together.

Next, try to deal with the tenants' **fears.** People will be afraid of being evicted if they fight the landlord. Even if not expressed, these fears are there, so you had better try to bring them out and deal with them, or else you will find the tenants promising now but dropping out later when the action starts.

Explain to the tenants that while some tactics (such as the rent strike) involve a high risk of eviction, others (such as picketing) do not, if the group has a competent lawyer to protect it from retaliatory evictions (which are prohibited by law). It will be up to the group to decide which tactics to use, after a lawyer comes to talk to them. Explain that no action will be taken until the group is ready, having first figured out a strategy, elected leaders, made work assignments, and lined up legal representation and community support. Tell them, however, that there is always some risk of eviction or rent raise, and if anyone is not willing to take it, he had better drop out now so the others don't depend on him.

From the very beginning, try to deal with the problem of internal dissension. Among the group, there are very likely to be feuds, jealousies, and even racial and ethnic prejudices. Try to bring these out in the open and resolve them as soon as possible, or else they will keep the group from working together when the going gets tough.

3. SETTING UP THE ORGANIZATION

At the first meeting, if you feel that the tenants have the qualities needed to take on the landlord, set up the organization of the tenant union. You might elect officers, including a president, vice president, secretary and treasurer. Or, you might elect a "steering committee" of four or five members (with a chairman) to be responsible for running things.

In setting up an organization, the most important thing is to see that there is a definite person responsible for each job which is important to the group. Here are some of the jobs that will need to be done: (1) line up a lawyer, (2) coordinate publicity, (3) get support from other groups, (4) handle the finances, (5) coordinate communication among the tenants (set up further meetings, contact people, etc.), (6) draw up demands and run negotiations, (7) gather information on the landlord. Each of these jobs can be assigned to a committee chairman, or they can be handled by certain officers. The actual work on these jobs should be done by as many people as possible, so everyone feels involved and no one feels overburdened. But make sure that there is one person responsible for seeing that each job gets done, and that the chairman or president is responsible for seeing that they get the job done.

Before adjourning the first meeting, the group should (1) select a name (for example, "540 Alcatraz Ave. Tenants' Union"), (2) decide the time and place of the second meeting, and (3) assign to specific people the jobs needed to be done before the second meeting, such as lining up a lawyer and contacting other tenants.

4. THE SECOND MEETING

The second meeting of the tenant union should be devoted to planning a strategy. Get some agreement on what are the most serious problems the tenants want resolved. Then have your "information" chairman report on what he found out about the landlord and to which tactics the landlord might be most vulnerable. Then

146

the lawyer should explain the possible consequences of using certain tactics and what he can do to protect the tenants.

Make sure that both the lawyer and the tenants understand that the lawyer is there only give advice and to help protect the tenants. He is not there to make decisions for the group. Before the meeting, your lawyer might benefit from reading Tenant Union Guide for Legal Services Attorneys, which appears in the **Handbook on Housing Law,** Volume II (Prentice-Hall, 1970), available at a law library. Also, see that tenants do not ask the lawyer to help solve their individual problems. He is there for the group, not for individuals, and if people fall back into an "individual" rather than "group" way of trying to solve landlord problems, the tenant union will fail.

Then the group should formulate a strategy. Make sure that there is general agreement with whatever strategy you decide on. A simple majority vote will not do if there is strong minority feeling opposed to it.

After the strategy is formulated, make specific work assignments to specific people, with deadlines for reporting to the chairman or the group that the job is done.

5. CONTACT OTHER GROUPS

Whatever strategy you decide on, you should try as soon as possible to get support from other groups in the community. Churches, labor unions, political clubs and social clubs can furnish money, publicity, political influence and moral support. Ask each tenant what groups he has contacts with which might help.

Be sure to contact groups which are concerned with tenants' rights. Some cities now have city-wide tenant associations. They can furnish technical advice as well as publicity and moral support.

You should also contact the National Tenants' Organization. NTO is located at 425 13th Street, N.W., Washington, D.C. 20004. It is made up of tenant unions from all over the country. NTO holds regional and national conferences where tenant organizers come and explain how to deal with specific problems. It also sends out a monthly newsletter, called "Tenants Outlook," which tells what tenant groups around the country are doing. The newsletter may give your tenant union some good ideas.

6. HOW MANY TENANTS DO YOU NEED BEFORE ACTING?

There is no set number. Sometimes only a few tenants will join initially, but many others may come in when the word spreads that the group is doing something and not just talking. If you cannot get a lot of people at first, try to get some "key" people who will influence others and bring them in later.

Obviously, the more tenants you have with you the more pressure the landlord will feel, so try to get as many tenants as you can in your tenant union.

C. GETTING INFORMATION ON THE LANDLORD

In order to find out how to deal with the landlord, you will need information on him. Sometimes you need to find out who the owner is. You should try to find out what his financial situation is like to see where he is most vulnerable. You need to know something about his personality before you negotiate with him.

Here are some sources of information you might check out.

1. TAX ASSESSOR'S OFFICE

The City or County Tax Assessor estimates the value of each

piece of property and keeps a record of to whom the tax bill is sent and who pays the taxes. This information is kept according to address, so you can obtain it without first knowing the name of the owner.

This can help you identify the real owner. Usually he is the one who pays the taxes. If not, then investigating the person who does pay the tax can lead you to the real owner.

If taxes have not been paid, this indicates either the landlord's poor financial condition or possibly his intent to abandon the building to the city or county.

The amount of the tax is a significant part of the landlord's expense in running the building. You may want to know this for negotiations.

Some assessors keep an alphabetical list of people who pay property taxes, specifying each piece of property on which they pay taxes. This can tell you how much property the landlord owns in the city or county and where it is. If he has other rental buildings, talk to the tenants there and see if they are interested in joining your effort. This can really help you increase the pressure on the landlord.

2. LOCAL REAL ESTATE OFFICES

For income tax reasons, slum buildings are put up for sale rather frequently, usually six to ten years after purchase. There is a fair chance that, at any given time, your building will be on the market.

You might send some substantial-looking person into a local real estate office to ask if the building is for sale and express interest in buying it. The real estate agent might furnish him some very helpful information concerning the building, especially information relating to income and expenses. While this information may be slanted to make the building seem more profitable than it is, this bias should make the figures useful to rebut the landlord's inevitable complaints that he is suffering financially from the building.

149

3. HOUSING CODE INSPECTION DEPARTMENTS

The city or county housing or building inspection department can be a source of information as to the condition of the building and the landlord's efforts (or lack of them) to repair.

First, since he must obtain a permit to make alterations in the building, you can find out when he last made substantial repairs and what he planned to do.

Second, find out when the agency last inspected the building and whether the violations were corrected. This documentation can be useful later for publicity or in court.

Also, find out if they have recorded any complaints by tenants. This can build your case that the tenants have long been concerned about the landlord's failure to repair and are not just creating this issue.

Since the law is unclear as to whether they are required to show you these things, it may help to try to find a sympathetic building inspector.

4. OTHER SOURCES OF INFORMATION

If you want to do a thorough job, here are some other sources of information you might check out:

a. County Recorder's Office

Here, if you know the name of the present owner, you can find out names of prior owners and who has mortgages, deeds of trust, or liens on the property.

b. Title Insurance Companies

They can tell you everything about the ownership of the property, including mortgages, etc. They usually charge for their services, but some people (such as attorneys who do real estate work) can often get information from title companies for nothing.

c. State Corporations Commissioner

If the building is owned by a corporation, they might tell you who runs the corporation.

d. Newspapers

A look through the local newspaper's "morgue" can sometimes produce good information on a landlord. A reporter who has covered the neighborhood for some time might also be helpful.

e. Ex-Managers and Former Tenants

These people may tell you how the landlord has treated people in the past. Since they are out, they have nothing to lose, and if they were mistreated by the landlord, they may be willing to help.

D. TACTICS

1. PETITION THE LANDLORD

The first thing you might do is draw up a petition which sets out your complaints and demands and give it to the landlord.

The petition should be worded politely but firmly. Remember that it might later get into the hands of other people, such as the newspapers or the courts, so you want to sound reasonable, even if the landlord deserves something stronger.

The demands should be clearly set out, and there should be a final demand for a response or a meeting by a specific time (such as a week later). Although it is probably not wise to set out at this point exactly what you intend to do if he is not cooperative (since you want to leave your options open until you are ready to act), the petition should carry the clear implication that the group means business.

It is usually better if all the tenants in the group sign the petition. This lets the landlord know that the people are united and serious enough about this to sign their names and risk possible reprisals. It also tends to make the people feel more committed.

The petition is a useful starting tactic, no matter what else you later decide to do. It forces the group to stop talking about general problems and decide what issues it will focus on. Often it will scare the landlord into submitting to some or all demands. Even if it doesn't, the landlord's response will give you an idea of how to deal with him in the future. Also, if you petition, you can later tell the newspapers, courts, and other groups that you tried to talk to him before you had to resort to your pressure tactics.

2. CALL THE CODE INSPECTOR

Calling the code inspectors and asking for an inspection of the building can be useful for several purposes.

First, an inspection which results in a report that there are violations shows that the tenants have legitimate grievances and are not just making things up to cause trouble or withhold rent. This can help gain public support and impress the courts.

Second, if you end up in court, you have the inspector available as a neutral, expert witness who can testify as to conditions in the building.

Third, an inspection which results in an order from the agency that the landlord make repairs may get him to fix the place, for otherwise the agency might have it condemned. Many sophisticated landlords, however, know how to handle the agency so as to avoid making repairs until the last possible moment. They are friendly with the inspectors, know how to take appeals and get extensions, and perhaps will get the agency to hold off by doing a few things and saying he is "working on" the others. He is less likely to get away with this where there are serious health hazards, such as rats or no heat. If you have these problems, call the Health Department rather than the Building Inspection Department, as they are generally more concerned about these issues.

There are some dangers in reporting code violations. First, if the building is really in bad shape, you may get too much action. The agency may condemn the building, or the landlord may decide it is cheaper to tear it down than fix it up. In either case, the tenants may be evicted.

Second, before calling the inspector, make sure that bad conditions were not caused by tenants, even in part. If they were, the inspector will probably find out about it. In that case, his report will usually do you more harm than good.

Finally, there is a danger of retaliatory eviction if the landlord finds out who reported the violations. Such evictions are prohibited by law,* and your lawyer should be able to protect you if the landlord tries this.

Before you call out a code inspector, try to find out if there is some inspector in the agency who will be sympathetic to what you are trying to accomplish. If there is, talk to him about these problems and see what he advises. He may be able to set things up so you get the most out of the inspection with the least risk.

3. PICKETING AND PUBLICITY

Slumlords don't like publicity, particularly if it affects their business or social lives. So it can be a very useful tactic.

Whenever you seek publicity by any means, make sure that you make specific charges and that what you are saying is true. This will keep you out of legal trouble and keep support on your side.

There are many ways to get publicity. Here are some of them:

Picketing at the building itself involves no travel time or expense, so it is easier to get tenants out to picket. This lets tenants, prospective tenants, and the neighborhood in general know what is going on, and it can help muster support. Picketing at the landlord's business office can put economic pressure on him by persuading his customers to stay away. This can be particularly effec-

---

*See Civil Code Section 1942.5; Moskovitz, Retaliatory Eviction—A New Doctrine in California, 46 California State Bar Journal 23 (1971).

tive when he is a rental agent or management company. A third possible location is the landlord's residence. This can be particularly effective if the landlord lives in an all white suburban neighborhood and the tenants are black or other minority.

Whenever you picket, be sure to contact the newspapers and television stations ahead of time. Their coverage will multiply the effect of your picketing.

Banners in the windows of tenants' apartments are another good way of letting tenants, prospective tenants, and the neighborhood know what is happening. Leaflets can also serve this purpose, and they are good to use when picketing, so people passing by (including reporters) can get the details of the dispute.

A press conference can be a good way of getting into all of the media at once. To get reporters and T.V. people to come, however, you will have to set it up at a time when they can come (that is, when nothing else of importance is happening) and call them personally, well ahead of time. Also, try to make the dispute sound dramatic. If conditions in the building are bad, have the press conference at the building and show the reporters the worst conditions.

If picketing or other publicity is hurting the landlord, he might file a law suit to try to stop it. He may ask the court to limit the number of pickets, stop distribution of material he claims is untrue, or stop the campaign entirely. The law on these issues is not clear, and what happens depends a lot on how the judge feels about it. Therefore, it is very helpful to have a lawyer to advice you and ready to represent you when you start a publicity campaign.

4. RENT STRIKES

The rent strike can be the most powerful tactic the tenants can use. It brings direct and immediate economic pressure to bear on the landlord. Few landlords are able to pay mortgage payments, property taxes, and other expenses from sources other than rents for long. If the landlord cannot break the rent strike quickly, he must come to the bargaining table.

Under a new California court decision,* **a rent strike is now legal in California, if** (1) the landlord has materially breached his "implied warranty of habitability" by failing to correct serious housing code violations, (2) tenants did not cause the violations, (3) the landlord was given notice of the violations and a reasonable time to correct them. How these requirements work and what happens if the landlord sues to evict rent strikers is more fully discussed in the section on rent withholding in Chapter 2.

If you decide to rent strike, there are some things you might do to minimize the danger of eviction.

---

*__Green__ v. **Superior Court**, 10 Cal. 3d. 616 (Jan. 15, 1974).

First, line up a good lawyer. If he fights the eviction action very hard and takes advantage of the rights you have,* it may take the landlord a long time to evict anyone, if he ever can. He might not be able to wait that long, so he may be willing to negotiate.

Second, inform the landlord that you are not simply pocketing the rent money, but are putting it in an "escrow account" which will be disposed of after the dispute is settled (by using it to make repairs, turning it over to the landlord or something else). This escrow account is **not** required by law. But it may impress the judge that you are not just trying to get something for nothing, so he may rule in your favor, or he may at least give you a chance to pay the rent to avoid eviction if he finds that the landlord did not materially breach his implied warranty of habitability. Also, if you dangle a large escrow account in front of a landlord, he will be more willing to deal with you than if the money is simply lost.

An escrow account can be set up as a bank savings account. Everyone deposits his rent in the account. For withdrawals, the signatures of both a tenant union officer and the tenant should be required. This assures each tenant that his money will not be spent without his consent. An easier way to set up an escrow is to rent a safe deposit box in a bank and have each tenant put a money order (or certified check) for the amount of the rent in the box as it comes due.

Whichever method you choose, make sure that every tenant follows it. If some tenants get a "free ride," morale will suffer badly and the group may easily fall apart.

Third, be sure to put together good evidence on the housing code violations. Take pictures (in color), get a housing code inspector or other expert to look at the place and have tenants ready to testify as to the conditions.

Finally, keep up your campaign for publicity and community support. This can help impress the judge that this is a very important issue.

---

*Have your lawyer see Moskovitz, Honigsberg and Finkelstein, **California Eviction Defense Manual** (Cont. Ed. Bar, 1971), and the **Tenant Union Guide for Legal Services Attorneys**, in Volume II of the Handbook in Housing Law (Prentice Hall, 1969).

5. REPAIR AND DEDUCT REMEDY

Another more modest form of rent strike may be permitted in California. The "repair and deduct" remedy, described in detail in Chapter 2, might be used by a group of tenants to make repairs costing no more than the total of the monthly rents of the tenants participating. For example, if the plumbing doesn't work and it will cost $800 to fix it, eight tenants might notify the landlord that they will pool their next month's rent of $100 each and have it fixed if he does not do so within a reasonable time. If he fails to do so, the tenants can have the work done, pay the bill, and deduct the amount from the next month's rent. There is presently no reported case in California where tenants have pooled their rents like this, but there seems to be nothing in Civil Code Sections 1941-1942.1 to prevent this.

Many times the threat of using this remedy will itself produce action.

6. LAW SUITS AGAINST THE LANDLORD

A law suit against the landlord can be another means of putting pressure on him so that he wants to negotiate with you. This might be done where he has locked someone out,* committed a retaliatory eviction or rent raise,** or refused to repair substantial housing code violations.***

A law suit puts the landlord on the defensive psychologically. He is in danger of having to pay substantial money damages. He will have to pay attorney's fees, which may be expensive.

If your law suit asks for "punitive damages," your attorney is entitled to find out the landlord's entire financial position, which

---

*Jordan v. Talbot, 55 Cal. 2d 597, 12 Cal. Rptr. 488 (1961).
**Aweeka v. Bonds, 20 Cal. App. 3d 278 (1971).
   But see Newby v. Alto Riviera Apts., 131 Cal. Rptr. 547 (1976).
***Quevedo v. Braga, 72 Cal. App. 3d Supp. 1 (1977).

he may not be anxious to reveal. Your attorney may also take the landlord's "deposition," requiring him to appear and answer questions which might make him uncomfortable.

You should be very careful about the effect on the tenant union of filing such a suit, however. Often when such a suit is filed, the tenants begin to rely too much on the law suit and the lawyer to solve their problems for them. They tend to stop their other efforts and the group gradually fades away. If this happens, even a victory in the law suit usually won't help the tenants much, since most of the tenants will probably move out before then. Be sure to tell the people (and the attorney) that the law suit is only one part of the campaign against the landlord to force him to negotiate with the tenant union. If they cannot accept this, then you probably should not file the suit.

7. LANDLORD'S COUNTERTACTICS

There are several things the landlord is likely to try to defeat your movement. He might file law suits against the tenants or try to get the police to stop the picketing. He might try to evict the leaders of the tenant union, or, thinking that if just one person is evicted the tenant union will collapse, he may try to evict one person he has good legal grounds to evict. He may try to pit certain tenants against others, making promises to some and blaming problems on others. A common tactic is to surprise the tenants by giving in to most of their demands right away with promises, then waiting for the group to fade away and then doing little or nothing.

The tenants should be aware of these possibilities and be ready to deal with them. They should remember to (1) always stick together and (2) don't relax until they have the final action they seek.

E. NEGOTIATIONS

Skill in negotiating is very important to maximize the results of your campaign against the landlord. Never forget, however, that the outcome will depend much more on who has the power outside the negotiating room, that is, what you can do to the landlord if he won't give you what you want and what you can give him if he will. The most skillful negotiator can't do much for powerless people, but inarticulate amateurs can often succeed when their opponent understands that they can and will use some real power if he does not give in.

1. PREPARATIONS

The tenant union should select a small negotiating team to speak for them.

These people should know as much as possible about the building, the tenants and the landlord. Psychologically, the landlord can gain control of the negotiating meeting if he overwhelms the tenants with his knowledge, so the tenants had better be prepared to keep up with him.

The negotiators should have a clear understanding of what their authority is, that is, what kind of deal the tenants will accept. The tenants should discuss their demands and tell the negotiators which demands are non-negotiable, which are "nice if they can get it," and which are expendable and can be traded off. In deciding this, the tenants must understand how strong they are and what they can realistically expect to get.

A role-playing session, with some tenants playing the landlord's role, can be very helpful to give the negotiators some experience.

The negotiators should have a proposed collective bargaining agreement ready at the meeting, so that they can get the landlord to commit himself in writing then and there. If there is nothing for him to sign, he might promise to sign something but change his mind later.

Finally, the negotiators should put together an overall strategy, knowing what they are after and how they are going to get there, so they can work together and not interfere with each other.

2. THE NEGOTIATING MEETING

The meeting should not take place at the landlord's office, where he will feel comfortable and the tenants intimidated. Have the meeting at the building or somewhere else in your neighborhood.

Have as many tenants as possible attend the meeting. This show of unity will impress the landlord and help the negotiators. It will also stimulate tenant interest and help strengthen the tenant union.

Make sure that the person you negotiate with is the owner or has the authority to make decisions binding on the owner. If this isn't made clear at the outset, they are wasting your time.

The negotiators should get across to the landlord—directly or subtly—what the union will do if negotiations break down and what they will give him if he comes to terms. On this latter point, you might tell the landlord that the tenant union and a collective bargaining agreement giving rights to tenants can increase tenant morale. This can cut down vandalism and vacancies and make rent payments more prompt.

One of the most important elements in negotiations is the psychological atmosphere. The landlord will try to be in control and keep the negotiators on the defensive. The negotiators should realize this and try to keep the landlord on the defensive.

F. THE COLLECTIVE BARGAINING AGREEMENT

The collective bargaining agreement is a key goal of the tenant union. Labor unions seek such agreements in order to firmly establish a continuing bargaining relationship with an employer, as well as to settle specific points of dispute. Tenant union collective bargaining agreements can do the same, so that the landlord has to deal with the union rather than the isolated tenant, and so the tenant can have the power of the union behind him whenever he has a grievance.

Remember, however, that the agreement will only be as effective as the continued willingness of the tenant union to make it effective. Even though the agreement is legally binding on the landlord, experience has shown that it will simply fade away unless the tenant union (or some larger neighborhood organization) is continually around as a "watchdog" to see that the landlord complies with it.

Here is a brief form* of collective bargaining agreement you may want to have adapted to fit your particular situation. Tell your lawyer what you want so he can write it in language that will be legally binding.

Take a copy of the signed agreement to the County Recorder's Office to have it recorded. This may prevent someone who buys the building from trying to avoid the agreement.

---

*A more extensive model agreement, with explanatory notes, appears in the **Tenant Union Guide**, in Volume II of the **Handbook on Housing Law** (Prentice-Hall, 1969).

COLLECTIVE BARGAINING AGREEMENT

I

Parties

The parties to this Agreement are _____,
hereinafter called "Landlord," and _____,
hereinafter called "Union." The property covered by this
Agreement is lcoated at _____.

II

Purpose

It is the general purpose of this agreement to provide a
better means of communication between Landlord and his
tenants, through Union, their bargaining agent, to assure a
continuous harmonious relationship and an orderly method
of resolving differences and grievances, which will result in
a stable tenancy, reduced expenses through greater tenant
concern, and a better community.

III

Dismissal of Pending Lawsuits

All lawsuits currently pending between Landlord and
Union or Landlord and any member of Union shall be dis-
missed, including the following: _____
_____.

IV

Recognition of Union

Landlord recognizes Union as the sole collective bargaining agent for its members who are tenants at the property covered by this Agreement on all matters relating to their tenancies, the building, and their dealings with Landlord in his capacity as owner.

V

Union Security

Landlord shall in no way discriminate against or take reprisals against any person because of his involvement or sympathy with Union. Nor shall Landlord promise or give any benefits to any person conditioned on such person's quitting, failing to join, or refusing to assist Union in any way.

VI

Tenant Responsibilities

Union agrees and recognizes that each tenant has certain obligations and responsibilities, including the following, and Union agrees to take no action to discourage tenants from complying with these obligations and responsibilities:

1. To pay rent promptly when due (except where provided otherwise by law, this Agreement, or agreement between Landlord and a tenant);

2. To pay for or correct any damage to the premises or Landlord's furnishings caused by any intentional or negligent act of a tenant or any person occupying the premises with his permission, excepting damage due to normal wear and tear;

3. To place his garbage and refuse inside the containers provided therefor;

4. To refrain from acts which unduly disturb his neighbors;

5. To obey all state and local laws and regulations relating to the occupancy of residential property;

6. To comply with his obligations under his lease or rental agreement.

VII

Leases [or Rental Agreements]

A standard form Model Lease [or Model Rental Agreement]* is attached to this Agreement and labelled "Exhibit A."

Within seven days of this Agreement, Landlord shall offer to sign such Model with each tenant who is a member of Union. Landlord shall make the same offer to each new member of Union with seven days of being notified of such membership by Union.

The provisions of this Agreement shall be considered incorporated into and a part of each such Model signed.

VIII

Rents

1. *Rents.* The following monthly rentals shall apply to the following units:

---

*See Chapter 1 for a Model to use.

2. *Appliances*. Landlord shall, without extra charge, furnish every apartment with a satisfactory stove and refrigerator, which he shall maintain in good working order.

3. *Utilities*. Landlord shall provide and pay for the following utilities, without adding to the monthly rent: gas, electricity, water, garbage collection, trash removal and sewer charges.

4. *Late Charges*. No late charges or fines shall be imposed.

5. *Rent Increases*. There shall be no rent increases during the term of this agreement.

6. *Back Rents*. Back rents in the amount of_____ now held by Union shall be disposed of as follows:_____

_____.

IX

Repairs and Maintenance

1. *Maintenance*. Landlord shall maintain the building and grounds in a decent, safe and sanitary condition, and shall comply with all state and local laws, regulations and ordinances concerning the maintenance of residential property. In addition, as specific maintenance problems have arisen in the past, Landlord specifically agrees to provide the following maintenance services:

[*Example*] (a) check the coin-operated washing machine and dryer at least once a week to see that they are in good operating condition;

(b) repair broken mailboxes upon notice by affected tenants.

2. *Security.* Landlord shall take reasonable measures to maintain security in the building and grounds to protect the tenants and their guests from burglary, robbery and other crimes.

3. *Repairs.* Landlord shall complete the following repairs by the following dates:

Repair	Date

4. *Failure to Comply.* Union shall have the right to inspect the building at reasonable times to insure compliance with this Section. If any repair is not completed by the date specified, or if Landlord fails to comply with any maintenance duty for seven days or longer, the tenants of the building may thereafter, until completion of repairs or resumption of maintenance, pay their rent into a bank account held by Union. Union shall use the money to make the repairs or perform the maintenance, remitting the balance to Landlord after repairs are completed and maintenance resumed. This remedy shall be in addition to any remedies provided by law or contract for tenants receiving inadequate mainenance or repair.

X

Grievance Procedure

1. The term "grievance" shall mean any dispute between Landlord and a tenant or between Landlord and Union involving the interpretation, application, or coverage of this

Agreement or any lease or rental agreement, except that any claim for personal injuries exceeding $500 shall not be considered a "grievance" subject to this procedure.

2. Any tenant having a grievance may present his grievance, by himself or through Union, to Landlord or his agent.

3. If the grievance has not been resolved to the satisfaction of the tenant within ten days after being presented, a grievance meeting shall be held between the tenant, Union, and Landlord within the next five days, or as soon thereafter as the parties may agree. At such meeting, the parties shall attempt to resolve the grievance to everyone's satisfaction.

4. If Landlord has a grievance against any tenant, or against Union, he may present such grievance to Union, which shall attempt to resolve the grievance as soon as possible.

5. If Landlord's grievance has not been resolved to his satisfaction within ten days after it has been presented to Union, the grievance meeting provisions subsection 3 above shall apply.

6. If the grievance meeting produces no resolution of the grievance, the aggrieved party may then file suit in any court of the competent jurisdiction for final determination of the matter in dispute.*

---

*For a grievance procedure containing a provision for arbitration by a neutral arbitrator before going to court, see the **Tenant Union Guide,** in Volume II of the **Handbook on Housing Law** (Prentice-Hall, 1969).

XI

Enforcement

The provisions of this Agreement may be enforced through appropriate legal action by Landlord, Union, or any affected person. As the amount of damages attributable to violation of any provision of this Agreement may be difficult to ascertain, the parties agree that these provisions may be specifically enforced by any appropriate court.

XII

Severability

In the event that any provision of this Agreement is deemed invalid by any court of law, it is mutually agreed that such determination shall not affect any other provisions of this Agreement and the Agreement shall remain binding on all parties hereto.

XIII

Union's Right to Information

In order to enable Union to maintain a continuing interest in the present and future condition of the building and to adequately represent the interests of the tenants, Landlord shall furnish Union with information and allow Union to examine Landlord's records and books, upon reasonable notice by Union, relating to the following matters:

1. expenses of maintaining the building;

2. income received from the building,

3. all other financial information relating to the building, including mortgages or deeds of trust on the building, and

4. all taxes affected by the building.

XIV

Duration

This Agreement shall remain in full force and effect from the date it is signed by both Landlord and Union and until _____, 19___.

On _____, 19___ , Landlord and Union shall begin negotiations for a new agreement to go into effect at the expiration of this Agreement. Such negotiations shall continue in good faith until a new agreement is reached or this Agreement expires.

WHEREFORE, We, the undersigned, do hereby execute and agree to this Agreement.

For the Landlord: *For the Union:*

1. _____   1. _____
      (signature)   (signature)

   _____   _____
      (title)   (title)

   _____   _____
   (date of signature)   (date of signature)

2, _____   2. _____
      (signature)   (signature)

   _____   _____
      (title)   (title)

   _____   _____
   (date of signature)   (date of signature)

G. CONDOMINIUM CONVERSIONS

Converting buildings from rental properties to condominiums was unusual several years ago. Now, however, the general shortage of new homes, coupled with favorable tax laws, has created a condominium boom. Whether condominium ownership makes sense as an abstract principle need not concern us here. We are concerned with the tenants of existing rental properties who are unable or unwilling to pay large sums of money to purchase their units.

One day the mailman delivers an identical letter to all the tenants in a multi-unit building. The owner it seems has decided to convert the building from rental units to an owner occupied condominium. Everyone will have to either buy their apartment and a share of the common space such as halls and grounds, or move out. Those with leases must leave when they run out, and those with month to month tenancies under a written rental agreement must leave in thirty days. The letter concludes politely that the owners hope that they have caused no inconvenience and are sure that many tenants will welcome this opportunity to buy their units at the rock bottom price of $45,000 each.*

Is there anything a tenant can do in the above situation if he wants neither to move or buy his unit? Can't the landlord do pretty much what he wants? At first impression it it would seem that the law favors the landlord and that the tenant is in a hopeless position, but don't give up too fast. Some very determined tenants in New York and San Francisco have proved that tenants acting together are not powerless.

Early in 1974 the tenants of the Parkmerced project in San Francisco learned that the new owner planned to convert to a condominium. The residents of the 3400 units could buy the units or get out. They wanted to do neither and, like similar groups of tenants in New York City, they haven't. Among other things they got the Board of Supervisors of San Francisco County to pass an ordinance prohibiting the conversion of buildings with more than twenty-five units until rules and regulations governing conversion could be adopted. Working

---

*To familiarize yourself with the enemy's intelligence, see **How To Convert Apartments to Condominiums**, California Real Estate Association, 1973.

through their newly formed and very efficient residents organization the tenants have drafted and gotten the San Francisco Board of Supervisors to pass a comprehensive set of condominium conversion rules. Most important among these is the requirement that 35% of the tenants living in any building or project with more than 50 units must approve the conversion from rental units to condominium ownership before the conversion can take place. The ordinance, which is quite lengthy, also calls for public hearings, notice requirements to tenants and the making of 10% of the units available for low and moderate income families if government subsidies are available.

The Parkmerced tenants, many of whom are over sixty years of age, have set up a tenants organization to which the majority of tenants pay small monthly dues. They have a newsletter, a legal committee, a publicity committee etc. They have been quite successful in forming alliances with other community groups concerned about tenants problems. For more information write:

George McCadden
PARKMERCED RESIDENTS ORGANIZATION
7 Diaz Avenue
San Francisco, California 94132

In 1976, a new state law was enacted which provides that a city or county shall not approve a condominium conversion unless (1) each tenant was given 120 days written notice of the intent to convert prior to termination of tenancy due to the conversion, and (2) each tenant was given the first right to buy his or her apartment on at least the same terms that the apartment will be offered to the general public.*

So if you are faced with a condominium conversion, don't give up. Re-read this chapter and get together with your neighbors and organize. You will probably find that the other tenants in your city face similar situations. Together you may be able to exert enough political pressure to save your home.

---

*Government Code section 66247.I.

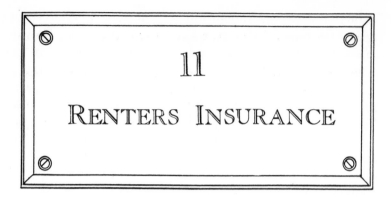

11

RENTERS INSURANCE

Attitudes toward insurance vary — some people wouldn't be without it while others consider it a giant rip-off. Our job is not to argue this question one way or the other, but to tell you how renters insurance works.

Renters insurance is a package of several types of insurance designed to cover tenants from more than one risk. Different insurance companies put slightly different things in their packages, both as to types of coverage, dollar amounts of coverage and especially deductible clauses. There is nothing we can tell you here that will substitute for your shopping around and comparing policies and prices. They do vary. It's a good idea to talk to friends and see if they are happy with their insurance, but realize that prices for renters insurance can be very different depending upon where you live. In certain high theft areas it is almost unattainable.

The average renters policy covers you against losses to your belongings occurring as a result of fire and theft up to the amount stated on the face of the policy which is often $5,000, $10,000 or $25,000. As thefts have become more common, most policies have included "deductible" amounts of $50, $100, or even $500. This means that if you are burgled, you collect from the insurance company only for the amount of your loss over and above the "deductible" clause.

Many renters policies completely exclude certain property from theft coverage, including cash, credit cards, pets, etc., while others limit the amount of cash covered to $100, the value of manuscripts to $1,000 and jewelry and furs to $500. Make sure your policy covers what you think it does. If it doesn't, check out the policies of other companies. As a general rule you can get whatever coverage you want if you are willing to pay for it.

In addition to fire and theft coverage most renters policies give you, and your family living with you, personal liability coverage to a certain amount stated in the policy. This means that if you directly injure someone (you hit them on the head with a golf ball), they are injured on the rental property that you occupy through your negligence (they slip on a broken front step), or you damage their belongings (your garden hose floods the neighbor's cactus garden), you are covered. There are a lot of exclusions to personal liability coverage, important among them being any damage you do with a motor vehicle, boat or through your business.

IMPORTANT: Your landlord's "homeowners" insurance won't cover you. Even if you live in a duplex with your landlord and the landlord has a "homeowners" policy, this policy won't protect your belongings if there is a fire or theft. Of course, if you suffer a loss as a result of your landlord's negligence, you may have a valid claim against him. Some large landlords have insurance to specifically protect against this sort of risk.

If you have a loss, be sure your insurance company treats you fairly. You are entitled to the present fair market value (not the replacement cost) of anything stolen or destroyed by fire or any other hazard covered by the policy after the deductible amount of the policy is subtracted. If the company won't pay you a fair amount, consider taking the dispute to Small Claims Court if it is for $500 or less. If the loss is a major one, you might consider seeing a lawyer, but agree to pay the lawyer only a percentage of what he or she can recover over and above what the insurance company offers you without the lawyer's help.

INDEX

ABOUT THE AUTHORS

MYRON MOSKOVITZ is a native San Franciscan who received his law degree (with honors) from the University of California in Berkeley in 1964. Since then, he has served as a law clerk for the California Supreme Court, directed the Marysville office of California Rural Legal Assistance, and was the Chief Attorney of the National Housing Law Project in Berkeley. He has written many articles and a book on tenants' rights for lawyers, and he has won several important cases establishing new rights for tenants. He is now a law professor at Golden Gate University, in San Francisco, and was appointed by Governor Brown to be Chairman of the State's Commission of Housing and Community. Development.

RALPH WARNER lives in Berkeley, California. He is an attorney, but spends most of his time writing, lecturing and consulting with the aim of getting people to better understand their legal system. A graduate of Princeton University and Boalt Hall School of Law, Ralph is the former Deputy Director of the Contra Costa Legal Service Foundation. Earlier, he was legal assistant to Chief Judge Richard Chambers of the U.S. Court of Appeals. Warner is co-author of THE PEOPLE'S GUIDE TO CALIFORNIA MARRIAGE LAW, and SEX, LIVING TOGETHER AND THE LAW, A Legal Guide For Unmarried Couples and Groups. He is also a founder of the Wave Project Do Your Own Divorce Centers. When not at work trying to debunk lawyers and their stranglehold on legal information, he enjoys climbing mountains, floating down rivers and tripping about the world.

CHARLES E. SHERMAN has served as a Deputy District Attorney (Los Angeles and Contra Costa Counties), a Senior Attorney in Contra Costa Legal Services, and has been in private practice. He is best known as the author of HOW TO DO· YOUR OWN DI-VORCE, and founder of The Wave Project's Do Your Own Divorce Centers. He is also a co-author of PROTECT YOUR HOME WITH A DECLARATION OF HOMESTEAD.

TONI LYNNE IHARA, the editor is an attorney, and recent graduate of the School of Law at the University of California at Davis. She has worked for the Legal Aid Society of Alameda County and is the co-author of PROTECT YOUR HOME WITH A DECLARATION OF HOMESTEAD and THE PEOPLE'S GUIDE TO CALIFORNIA MARRIAGE LAW. She loves mountains, oceans and the laughter of the spheres.

Other Nolo Books

CALIFORNIA DEBTORS' HANDBOOK - BILLPAYERS' RIGHTS (California Edition): Everyone over their heads in debt will benefit by reading this book. Information on dealing with wage attachments, repossessions, bankruptcy, collection agencies, etc. "Almost a case history of how every debt situation was solved without money and without pain to the debtor." ---San Francisco Examiner $4.95

THE LIVING TOGETHER KIT: Legal information on buying and renting property, credit, having children, dealing with a former spouse, sex laws, death, etc. Includes a special chapter for gay couples. Good in all 50 states. Contains tear-out living together contracts and sample paternity statements and will. By Toni Ihara and Ralph Warner. $8.95

HOW TO CHANGE YOUR NAME (California Edition): Changing your name is cheap and easy. This book comes complete with all the forms you need to do it yourself. Full information on women's name problems with special attention to women who want to retain, or return to, their own name after marriage or divorce. This book is primarily valuable to Californians. $5.95

HOW TO DO YOUR OWN DIVORCE IN CALIFORNIA: This famous book revolutionized the divorce field by making it clear and simple to the layperson. Tells you the practical things you need to think about and gives information and advice on making your various decisions. Shows exactly how to do your own. Over 200,000 copies in print have saved Californians more than $15 million in attorney fees. (California only) $5.95

PROTECT YOUR HOME WITH A DECLARATION OF HOMESTEAD: Your home can be protected from your creditors up to $30,000 under California law only if you file a homestead. Here we tell you how to do it cheaply, easily and legally. All forms are contained in the book. An invaluable gift for the new homeowner. Third Edition. $4.95

HOW TO FORM YOUR OWN CALIFORNIA CORPORATION: This book, by California attorney Anthony Mancuso, includes tear-out Articles, By-laws, minutes and stock certificates and all the instructions necessary to set up your own small California corporation. Takes advantage of the 1977 Corporation law. For profit corporations only. (Second Edition) $12.00

THE PEOPLE'S GUIDE TO CALIFORNIA MARRIAGE LAW (Complete with sample marriage contracts): By California attorneys Ralph Warner and Toni Ihara. Information of benefit to every married couple and to those thinking of getting married, including a discussion of community and separate property, names, debts, children, sex, buying a house, etc. Also contains a simple will, probate avoidance information and an explanation of inheritance and gift taxes. A perfect wedding or anniversary present. $5.95

LANDLORDING: A practical guide for the conscientious landlord and landlady. Covers repairs, maintenance, getting good tenants, how to do your own eviction with the necessary legal forms, record keeping and taxes. "A step-by-step guide to acquisition of business sense." ---San Diego Tribune. This is a large book, 8½ x 11, 253 pages, produced by Express Press and distributed by Nolo Press.
$12.50

SMALL TIME OPERATOR: How to start your own small business, keep your books, pay your taxes and stay out of trouble. Includes a year's supply of ledgers and worksheets. This book is for people who have an idea, a skill or a trade, and the desire to make their living working for themselves. By Bernard Kamoroff, C.P.A. Distributed by Nolo Press.
$6.95

HOW TO COLLECT YOUR CHILD SUPPORT AND ALIMONY: An experienced attorney and collector tell you step-by-step how to collect all that back support. Includes sections on how to find people and their property as well as what to do when you do find them. This is one of the most valuable books we have ever published. There has never been one like it.
$7.95

PROBATE AND TAXES: All Californians concerned with saving money on taxes and probate fees will want to read this book. Contains detailed information on state and federal inheritance taxes with many, many saving hints. Written by attorney Ian McPhail and distributed by Nolo Press.
$5.95

EVERYBODY'S GUIDE TO SMALL CLAIMS COURT: The essence of bringing a successful case in Small Claims Court is preparation. This book, written by attorney Ralph Warner with numerous examples, sample testimony, etc., shows you how to prepare in detail. Ralph also discusses who and how to sue and what to do once you have your judgment.
$5.95

CALIFORNIA NON-PROFIT CORPORATION BOOK: A complete step-by-step guide on how to form your own non-profit corporation in California. Complete with information on how to get section 501(c)(3) tax exempt status. By attorney Anthony Mancuso.
$12.00

To order books, send check or money order (include 6% tax and 50¢ per book for postage and handling) to:

NOLO PRESS
Box 544
Occidental, California 95465
(707) 874-3105

UPS AND DOWNS
A journal of wilderness love and lovers

By Toni Ihara and Ralph Warner

Here you will find Toni and Ralph living naked on a Polynesian beach, lost in the High Sierra snow, and facing a grizzly bear in the Canadian north.

"A 20th-century commentary in the John Muir tradition. For both novices and old hands this work is as essential to a back-packing collection as trail guides and how-to's." —Booklegger Magazine

NOLO PRESS
Box 544, Occidental, Calif. 95465

The Treasure of LOST DRAGON CASTLE & other stories

Especially for ages 6-13
By Ralph Warner and Toni Ihara

Silly, delightful detective-adventure stories featuring Albert Muldoon as the incompetent detective, Renfro as his improbable sidekick, and Clem as the great detective dog who makes it all come out O.K. in the end. Lots of kids have told us that this is "my best book ever".

"Muldoon is a great goofy goon..."

Damon Ray Geddins, 6th Grade

"I couldn't put it down. The part about all the bats and stuff in the castle is neat. An all around funny story."

Jonathan Eliasberg, 5th Grade

$3.50